God Still Calls

God Still Calls
Discerning God's
Direction for Service

Mark A. Maddix and Stephen Riley,
Editors

BEACON HILL PRESS
OF KANSAS CITY

Cover Design: Sherwin Schwartzrock
Interior Design: Sharon Page

Library of Congress Cataloging-in-Publication Data
Names: Maddix, Mark A., 1965- editor. | Riley, Stephen, 1974- editor.
Title: God still calls : discerning God's direction for service / Mark A. Maddix and Stephen Riley, editors.
Description: Kansas City, MO : Beacon Hill Press of Kansas City, [2017] |
   Includes bibliographical references.
Identifiers: LCCN 2016029995 | ISBN 9780834136212 (pbk.)
Subjects: LCSH: Clergy—Office. | Vocation—Christianity. | Service (Theology) |
Christian leadership.
Classification: LCC BV660.3 .G63 2017 | DDC 253/.2—dc23 LC record available at https://lccn.loc.gov/2016029995

10 9 8 7 6 5 4 3 2 1

 # Contributors

Rev. Phillip Antilla, Senior Pastor, Ashland First United Methodist Church, Ashland, Oregon

Rev. Gabriel J. Benjiman, Pastor and Africa Nazarene Regional Educational Coordinator, Morningside Community Church of the Nazarene, Durban, South Africa

Rev. Nick Bollinger, Owner, Junction Coffee, Oklahoma City, Oklahoma

Rev. Gideon de Jong, Associate Pastor, Saint John's Church of the Nazarene, Berlin, Germany

Rev. Rod DeVore, Family Involvement Specialist, Metro Nashville Public Schools, Nashville, Tennessee

Rev. Dave and Rev. Carolita Fraley, Former Missionaries to France and Current Pastors, Canyon Hill Church of the Nazarene, Caldwell, Idaho

Rev. Shawna Songer Gaines, Chaplain, Trevecca Nazarene University and Rev. Dr. Timothy R. Gaines, Assistant Professor of Religion, Trevecca Nazarene University, Nashville, Tennessee

Rev. Dr. Nina Griggs Gunter, General Superintendent Emeritus, Church of the Nazarene, Nashville, Tennessee

Rev. John Haines, Eurasia Regional Education Coordinator, Church of the Nazarene, Schaffhausen, Switzerland

Rev. Jerry Hull, Pastor and Professor Emeritus of Social Work, Northwest Nazarene University, Nampa, Idaho

Rev. Stephanie Johnson, Co-Pastor, Kennewick Church of the Nazarene, Kennewick, Washington

Rev. Simon Jothi, President, South Asia Nazarene Bible College, Bangalore, India

Rev. Megan Krebs, Student, Nazarene Theological Seminary, Kansas City, Missouri

Rev. Cassandra Lara, Education Coordinator, Mother's Refuge, Independence, Missouri

Rev. Bob Luhn, Retired Pastor, Othello Church of the Nazarene, Othello, Washington

Rev. Dr. Jesse Middendorf, General Superintendent Emeritus, Church of the Nazarene, Overland Park, Kansas

Rev. Frank Lantei Mills, Pastor and District Superintendent, Church of the Nazarene Ghana North District, Ghana, Africa

Rev. Ignacio and Rev. Litzy Pesado, District Superintendent and Pastors, Church of the Nazarene Spain District and Barcelona Church of the Nazarene, Barcelona, Spain

Rev. Scott Shaw, District Superintendent, Church of the Nazarene Intermountain District, Nampa, Idaho

Rev. Jenna Redmond Stout, Candidate Development Coordinator, Nazarene Global Missions, Lenexa, Kansas

Rev. Joy Streight, Pastor, Castle Hills Church of the Nazarene, Boise, Idaho

Rev. Jay and Rev. Teanna Sunberg, Missionaries, Church of the Nazarene, Budapest, Hungary

Rev. Jennifer Roemhildt Tunehag, Independent Missions Consultant for Human Trafficking, Hässelby, Sweden

Rev. Andrew and Rev. Simone Twibell, Assistant District Superintendent, Church of the Nazarene Chicago Central District, Bourbonnais, Illinois

Rev. Ruben Villarreal, Pastor, ThornCreek Church of the Nazarene, Thornton, Colorado

Rev. Krystal Wigginton, Youth Pastor, Garden Grove Church of the Nazarene, Garden Grove, California

Rev. Mike Yost, Pastor, Longview Church of the Nazarene, Longview, Washington

Contents

God Still Calls

Mark A. Maddix

God still calls! God is still at work! God is on the move! God is calling men and women to serve the church and the kingdom of God. As reflected in the allegorical Christian novel *The Lion, the Witch, and the Wardrobe* (1950), Aslan is a great lion who is the king of Narnia. Narnia, in the time period of this novel, is experiencing a siege of the throne by the White Witch, who makes it always winter in Narnia—but never Christmas. Aslan is more than a lion in C. S. Lewis's great series; he is also a symbol of Jesus Christ. With the announcement from one of the beavers that "Aslan is on the move," the Narnians are reassured that the reign of the White Witch will not last forever. Aslan is coming to make things right. The hope of Aslan's movement is a reminder for readers that God continues to be on the move in our world. God is actively working in the world to bring about God's redemptive purposes, and God calls women and men to be ambassadors of the gospel.

This book is about a God who is on the move. God continues to call men and women into ministry in a variety of capacities. Some Christian leaders are concerned that many young people are not following God's call to serve in the ordained ministry. This is a legitimate concern, since many young adults are less concerned about the established church and more concerned about making a difference in the world. But reading these narratives of ministers of the gospel will persuade you that God has called and continues to call Christian leaders to full-time ministry. We also hope, as you read these narratives, that you will be able to relate to and identify with how these leaders discerned God's call in their lives. Some of the narratives speak of a direct call, some testify to the role of other Christians in affirming their call, and others indicate a confirmation by God of their gifts and abilities as they engaged in ministry. As you will see, God moves in the lives of people in a variety of ways in order to fulfill God's redemptive purpose in the world. In a time when it seems it is always winter and God isn't evident, God is on the move. God continues to lead the church to participate in the ushering in of the kingdom of God.

Categories of Vocational Callings

Talking about Christian vocation (summons or calling) can mean different things to different groups of people. This meaning has particular ramifications for the millennial generation, who have a much broader understanding of Christian vocation than previous generations. They are less likely to view their calling as a call to serve in ordained ministry and more likely to view it as a call to serve in areas of social justice, reconciliation, and mission. As you read through the stories in this book, you will see that many of our so-labeled *emergent* leaders use different language and terminology to articulate their call as compared to the *experienced* or *emeritus* leaders. This difference reflects a change in how they understand their call and how it is being implemented in their lives.

In order to give clarity to our understanding of calling, it is helpful to provide some categories regarding the meaning of Christian vocation.

First, we refer to a *general calling*, since all Christians are called to be faithful disciples and to fulfill their vocational mission in the world. All Christians are called to lives of discipleship and to be followers of Jesus Christ.

Second, there is what Doug Koskela refers to as the *missional calling*, which describes women and men who are called to serve in full-time ministries like para-church ministry, camps, inner-city missions, or music directors. These are non-ordained ministry positions and can include a variety of careers and professions. The term *missional calling* means that the specific guiding purpose God has for a person's life aligns with that person's gifts and passions. The missional calling takes time, prayer, and the involvement of the local community to discern God's will for the person being called.[1]

Third, there are women and men who are called to a *specific calling*, which refers to God's call to serve in a particular task or purpose connected with the office of ordained ministry. These are people whom the church has set apart as ordained clergy to proclaim the good news of the gospel and to administer the sacraments. When we think about those who are called to vocational ministry, we often think of our clergy.

These three categories provide a basis for understanding the different ways God calls. It is important to have a clear understanding of each category as we discern God's direction for our own lives and the call to serve in ministry.

---

1. Doug Koskela, *Calling and Clarity: Discovering What God Wants for Your Life* (Grand Rapids: Eerdmans, 2015), xiv.

General Calling

God calls all Christians to be ministers. Dallas Willard, in his book *The Great Omission*, argues that being a Christian means being a disciple of Jesus.[2] In other words, you cannot be a Christian and not be a disciple of Jesus. The Greek word for disciple is *doulos*, which means to be a slave or servant. All believers are called to be disciples and are, therefore, called to be ministers (*diakonos*) and to be engaged in service (*diakonia*). In the New Testament, the concept of *diakonos* is applied universally to all who are members of the Christian community. In the New Testament, ministry never signifies ecclesial office; rather, it refers to leaders' function of serving the church. Therefore, Christians as ministers of the gospel are called to serve Christ and the church. This is the vocation of all Christians.

Closely connected with the universal understanding that all Christians are called to be disciples is the historical understanding of the priesthood of all believers. The impact of the Protestant Reformation was the focus on everyone reading Scripture on their own (*sola scriptura*) without the interpretation of the priest. The result was that everyone became a "priest" and was on equal ground with the ordained priests. In other words, even though the office of ministry was retained for those who preached and administered the sacraments, it resulted in a greater sense of equality among Christian leaders.

The impact of the Reformation is particularly felt today with the development of emergent and postmodern forms of pastoral leadership that negate the importance of ordination and give greater focus to the priesthood of all believers. In reality, this is the crux of the problem we face today. On the one hand, we celebrate the fact that all Christians are engaged in ministry (Christian vocation). But on the other hand, the impact of this shift has resulted in a lower view

---

2. Dallas Willard, *The Great Omission: Reclaiming Jesus's Essential Teaching on Discipleship* (New York: HarperOne, 2014).

of the need for the office of ministry—for those called to ordained ministry. In reality we need both ordained clergy and laity to share in the priesthood of Christ. The whole church carries out the mission of restoring the created order to its proper relationship with itself and with God as creator.

When we think about the word *vocation*, we typically think of it in association with the word *career*. In essence, we think of our vocation as how we make a living. In reality, vocation (calling or summons) refers to the various ways in which God calls us to live. We have choices to make about how we use our time, our gifts, and our abilities.[3]

We affirm that God has called all Christians to live out their Christian vocation by using the specific gifts and abilities God has given them. God clearly articulates in Scripture that a general calling includes obedience to follow God and God's will for our lives. God calls all Christians to a life of faithful discipleship through loving God completely and loving our neighbors as ourselves. Historically, we have viewed this *general calling* as referring to those who are not called to a priestly role or ordained ministry. Those with a general calling are often referred to as *laity*. Laity play a significant role in the body of Christ as they live out their Christian vocation. We need all Christians in their particular professions to view those professions as their vocations, and to view their vocations as a means to serve Christ, the church, and the kingdom of God.

Missional Calling

Some Christians are called to serve a specific function in ministry as non-ordained ministers. They utilize their gifts and passions for a specific, God-called purpose. This missional calling, or call to full-time Christian service, may include a specific function such as serving as a music director, in a para-church ministry, at a camp, as

---

3. Koskela, *Calling and Clarity*, xiii.

a Christian school teacher, or at a nonprofit agency. The missional calling can include a wide range of full-time Christian or religious work but does not include ordained ministry.

Missional calling refers to the main contribution your life makes to the kingdom of God. It is the distinct direction in which you aim to spend the bulk of your time, gifts, and energy. It may include a particular major or career path, but at the heart of missional calling is to recognize your gifts, abilities, and passions. When people recognize their missional calling, they acknowledge that God has wired them to serve in a particular way over the course of a lifetime.[4] In essence, everyone has a missional calling, but it may take time to know and fully embrace. It requires continual prayer and seeking God's guidance through life's journeys, especially since the calling can adapt and change over time.

The benefit of Koskela's category of missional calling is that it helps those who sense God's call to serve in restoring clean water in Africa, engaging in prison reform, counseling hurt people, advocating for human equality, or working for justice for those being oppressed by human trafficking. Many young adults and emerging leaders resonate with this category of calling. They sense God calling them to give their lives to God's redemptive mission in the world.

Specific Calling

God calls some women and men to be set apart from the church to serve in *ordained ministry*. Like Moses, these women and men have a specific call from God. They are called to extend God's mission in the world through the proclamation of the Word, to administer the sacraments, and to provide leadership to the local church. Many young adults ask, "Why do I need to be ordained? Can't I do effective ministry without being ordained?" These are legitimate questions. One of the primary reasons for ordination is that God calls, but the

---

4. Koskela, *Calling and Clarity*, 2.

church ordains. The ordained office of ministry is the confirmation of God's call to ministerial leadership as stewards and proclaimers of the gospel of Jesus Christ. Ordination not only confirms a minister's commitment to the church; it also allows the church to affirm its commitment to the minister. Ordination gives ministers authority to preach the gospel. It is a spiritual and theological act of the church. Ordination is more than receiving a certificate or passing a qualifying exam; it is the church's acknowledgment that God calls and gifts certain women and men for ministerial leadership in the church.

The call to full-time, ordained ministry includes both an *internal* (inner) and *external* (church) calling. First, a specific call of God entails a deep sense of conviction that God is calling. This inner, or internal, calling may take time to mature and grow deeper in one's heart. God calls people in a variety of ways. For some the call is clear, even in an audible voice, while for others the inner calling needs to be nurtured and affirmed. An inner calling may be affirmed by involvement in ministry through such practices as leading worship, preaching, or leading a Bible study. It also might include an encouraging word from a member of one's local church. A call to ordained ministry requires an inner sense of calling in order to fulfill the call to serve the local church, the body of Christ. Often people run from this call out of fear of the complexities of pastoral ministry, but as indicated in this book, the call to ordained ministry is one of the greatest joys of life.

Here are some resources that can help you discern the inner call of God on your life:

- Prayer and Spiritual Disciplines. As you commune with God, the inner call becomes more evident. Are you connected with God on a regular basis?
- Desires, Gifts, and Passions. Do you believe this inner call is a deep passion of your heart? Do you sense that God has given you the gifts, abilities, and passion to serve in leadership in

the church? Do you have the qualifications of a minister as expressed in 1 Timothy 3:1–13 and Titus 1:6–9?

- Spiritual Assessment. You need to take inventory of your walk with the Lord before you decide to pursue ministry. Are you in a good place in your spiritual life?

Second, an internal call to ordained ministry is confirmed *externally* through the body of Christ. A call is not just between you and God; it includes the body of Christ. People in your local congregation may often sense your calling before you do. They know you have the gifts and abilities to serve in ministry, and their encouragement affirms what God has already been saying in your heart.

For example, when I was called to ministry, many people in my local church already had a sense that God was calling me. They were just waiting for me to respond in obedience. Once I responded in obedience, they gave me the opportunity to preach, which was an affirmation of my call to preach. The body of Christ plays an important role in affirming or not affirming a call to ministry. We believe God calls people to ordained ministry from within the local church, and it is the local church that affirms God's gifts and callings for ordained ministry.

Closely connected with the role the body of Christ plays in affirming a call is your relationship with mentors, professors, and pastors. These significant spiritual leaders know you and your gifts and abilities. They can speak into your life by praying for you and giving guidance to the discerning process of your call to ministry. The relationships you have with these leaders are another external group that can affirm your call to ministry.

Another external avenue of confirmation can include your family. This is especially true for those who are already married when they receive the call. The spouse, too, needs to sense God's leading in this process and needs to feel comfortable with your call to ministry. Often, one of the biggest struggles for those who feel called to ordained ministry can be their families. Ordained ministry may require moving from the comfortable confines of family support, which often causes anxiety and stress. Also, some Christian parents do not want their children to go into ordained ministry. They want them to be in a profession that can support them financially and provide a more secure future.

As you consider and reflect on whether you are specifically called to ordained ministry, consider your surroundings and ask yourself the following questions as you seek external affirmation for your internal call:

- Local Church. In what ways has a local church affirmed your inner call to ministry? What aspects of ministry connect with your gifts and passions?
- Mentors. Do pastors, professors, and mature Christians see God's gifts and abilities in you for ministry? In what ways have they spoken into your life?
- Family Members. Is your spouse supportive of your call to ministry? Are you willing to relocate if God calls you? Are your parents supportive of your call to ministry? If not, what steps need to be taken to address this concern?

Elder and Deacon

Different Christian denominations have a variety of offices of ordained ministry. Most recognize the office of ordained ministry as being set apart to fulfill the priestly role. In this book, the majority of essays are written by clergy in the Church of the Nazarene. The Church of the Nazarene as part of the broader evangelical community typically refers to ordained ministry in two categories, elder and deacon.

The ordained elder is a man or woman who has been set apart to minister by proclamation of the Word, administration of the sacraments, and leading a local church. The important distinction between the ordained elder and the deacon is the call to preaching ministry. Many elders serve as pastors, missionaries, youth pastors, chaplains, and educators.

The ordained deacon is a man or woman who is called to full-time ministry but is not called to the preaching ministry. Deacons may preach on occasion, but this isn't part of their primary ministry. Ordained deacons perform full-time roles in ministry such as teaching, worship ministry, compassionate ministry, Christian education, social work, and the like.

As you read through the narratives of God's call in this book, we hope you are able to discern the difference between God's calling as either elders or deacons. Both play significant roles in helping the church fulfill its mission to build up the body of Christ and to extend God's mission in the world. The chart below provides a summary of the three categories of ministry callings.

Categories of Ministry Calling

General Calling (Christians)	Missional Calling (Non-Ordained Ministry)	Specific Calling (Ordained Ministry)
• The call to be faithful disciples (doulos) • The call to be witnesses of the good news of the gospel • The call to love God and neighbor • The call to use your gifts and abilities as part of your vocation • The call to a life of obedience to God's will	• A distinct vocation that utilizes your gifts, abilities, and passions • Many Christians have a missional calling, but it may take time to nurture it • Missional call to serve in issues of social justice, human trafficking, or counseling • Full-time, non-ordained ministry (camp director, counselor, music director, etc.)	• An inner call of God that is confirmed by the body of Christ • A call to serve a local church in the capacity of pastor, chaplain, missionary, or related pastoral ministry • Set apart by the church to preach the Word, administer the sacraments, and lead the local church • Office of elder (preaching) or deacon

Conclusion

It is our hope that, as you read this book of call narratives, you will be able to discern the ways in which God is calling you to ministry. We hope to provide answers to your big questions, soothe your frustration, and offer you greater clarity. We believe God is still calling and that God is on the move. We acknowledge that God is developing a group of missionally driven leaders, with a clear sense of vocation, to make a difference in the world. This is a call every Christian should have, regardless of profession or career.

We have also written this book to provide examples of women and men who are giving their lives to ordained ministry. They are pastors, missionaries, and educators who have received an inner call from God that has been affirmed by a variety of external sources. They provide us with an example of the deep gratification that comes when you connect your gifts, graces, and abilities with God's call in your life. They illustrate the joy and satisfaction that comes as a minister of the gospel.

God still calls! God is on the move!

Discussion Questions

1. What is the ordained ministry, and how is it distinct from other calls to ministry?

2. What internal and external resources are needed to affirm an inner call to ministry? How have you consulted these resources?

3. In what ways has God affirmed your inner call to ministry?

4. Which of the three categories described in chapter 1 best expresses your call to ministry? In what ways do you sense that God is calling you into ministry?

Resources for Further Reading

Drury, Keith. *The Call of a Lifetime: Is the Ministry God's Plan for Your Life?* Indianapolis: Wesleyan Publishing House, 2003.

Garber, Steve. *Visions of Vocation: Common Grace for the Common Good.* Downers Grove, IL: InterVarsity Press, 2014.

Koskela, Doug. *Calling and Clarity: Discovering What God Wants for Your Life*. Grand Rapids: Eerdmans, 2015.

Tripp, Paul David. *Dangerous Calling: Confronting the Unique Challenges of Pastoral Ministry*. Wheaton, IL: Crossway, 2012.

Willimon, William H. *Calling and Character: Virtues of the Ordained Life*. Nashville: Abingdon Press, 2000.

Biblical Foundations of God's Calling
Stephen Riley

And God said, "Let there be light," and there was light. God called the light day . . .
Genesis 1:3, 5

As Jesus went on from there, he saw a man named Matthew sitting at the tax collector's booth. "Follow me," he told him, and Matthew got up and followed him.
Matthew 9:9

Themes of Scripture's Witness to God's Calling

From the first verses of Scripture, God has been calling. The first thing God does is call forth light. God calls the light "day" and ordains it for its particular purpose. This pattern is repeated throughout the first chapter of Genesis. At the end of the chapter, God calls forth humanity and ordains them to be "fruitful and increase in number; fill the earth and subdue it" (Genesis 1:28). Here, God calls humanity into a covenant relationship designed to bring forth care and foster well-being in the world. This well-being is often referred to as *shalom*, or wholeness, a state of existence where all creation can flourish as God intends.

Unfortunately, humanity's narrative has included frequent rejection of God's call to live into this covenant of *shalom*. The opposite of *shalom* is known as sin. Scripture clearly witnesses to the effects of sin, which brings creation to an existence of chaos and hopelessness. However, this hopeless existence is not the end. In the midst of chaos, Scripture witnesses that God graciously cares for us. Time and time again, God calls particular people to vocational tasks that help the people of God fulfill the covenant and return to *shalom*.

This chapter will explore the biblical witness to God's calling on humanity to work in covenant with God for the sake of this world. First, we will look at Scripture's witness to God's covenantal nature. God consistently calls humans into a covenantal relationship for the purpose of *shalom* in the world. Second, we will examine Scripture's witness that God calls all types of people to work in missional callings for the covenant. There is no single type of person God uses to help the community of faith accomplish *shalom*. Finally, we will observe that God calls certain people to a life of ordained ministry. Scripture tells how people in a number of locations and stages of life are called to help shape God's people for covenantal work. We often refer to this as vocational ministry. The question has been, and continues to be, are we willing to listen and respond?

God Works in Covenant with Humans

God is a God of covenant. This means that God calls humans into a relationship that requires a certain type of response, a way of being in the world that is consistent with the nature of the God who calls. This witness can be seen in the first chapters of Genesis, where God creates humanity in the image of God and then calls them to be fruitful, multiply, fill the earth, and have dominion over that which is in it. The language of this covenant, found in Genesis 1:26–28, is primarily a language reserved for kings, who were called to be caretakers of their people and their land. This caring for all creation, including vegetation, animals, and other humans is a part of bringing about *shalom*. In this case, *shalom* looks like well-being and wholeness—creation as it was intended. Scripture also gives witness that humanity has not always kept their end of the covenant. However, that has not stopped God from continuing to call. In fact, this initial call to covenant is not the only covenant witnessed in Scripture.

In the twelfth chapter of Genesis, God moves from a call to the whole of humanity to a call to a particular human family into a covenant relationship. God calls Abram and Sarai, later known as Abraham and Sarah, and promises to make them a great nation. Part of the purpose of this relationship is seen in Genesis 12:3, where God tells Abram that in him all nations will be blessed. In effect, God's covenant with this family is intended to bring about the blessing of all peoples as they move toward the land God has promised. This blessing is intended to be for the well-being, the *shalom*, of Abraham and his family as well as those surrounding them. Of course, the Abraham cycle, as well as the following narratives of Isaac, Jacob, and Joseph, tell an up-and-down pattern of Israel sometimes getting it right but often failing in their pursuit of the covenant. Despite Israel's failure, God is still faithful. God never fails the covenant or the people God has called into relationship.

Later, in Exodus, after Abraham's descendants have been enslaved for four hundred years, God delivers the Israelites from the house of slavery and brings them out into the plains of Sinai. There, God establishes a covenant with the people through Moses. In this covenant, the people are given stipulations that will set up the type of community they are called to be. In the nineteenth chapter of Exodus, God tells Moses that in this covenant the Israelites are called to be a "priestly kingdom and a holy nation." The idea of being a priestly kingdom means a people who are chosen to help others connect with God. To be holy means that Israel's purpose aligns with God's purpose. The point of being delivered from slavery is so Israel can be a particular type of community that influences the rest of the world. Their witness will show the nature of the relationship God wants to have with humanity as well as the relationships humans should enjoy with one another. In doing so, Israel's living out of their covenant with God will invite the nations to come, be blessed, and flourish in a world that reflects the original intent for creation.

Unfortunately, Scripture also gives witness that Israel does not always live into the reality of their covenant with God. Their historical and prophetic texts tell of their repeated failure to be a community of *shalom*. Leaders rise and fall, but few are able to lead the people in faithful observance of the covenant in ways that reflect the creation care and holy people the early texts reference. The prophets witness to God's deep desire that Israel live into the covenant reality, and as Israel fails to live into the covenant, the prophets proclaim God's message in an attempt to return Israel to God.

Thankfully, Israel's failure as a nation is not the final word about God's covenant calling. The New Testament witnesses to God's fullest revelation of the covenant in Jesus Christ. Though the nation of Israel waxes and wanes in the frame of history, God's covenantal nature does not. In Jesus, God once again calls humanity to enter into covenant for the sake of the world. The life, death, and resurrection of Jesus most clearly reveal the covenantal nature of a God who is reaching out to redeem all creation. In Jesus's life we see one who calls and accepts any who will follow him. He embodies a life of self-giving love, proclaims forgiveness of sin, heals the suffering and wounded, and offers reconciliation with God and fellow humans. In his death and resurrection, we see that death is truly defeated, the claims Jesus made were true, and the reign of God breaks in on the world. In Jesus, the covenant of God with humanity looks most fully like the *shalom* of the world God intends in the early narratives of Genesis.

The end of Scripture also witnesses to the hope that God will continue to work toward the summation of the covenant. While Revelation should not be read flatly or simply as prophecy about the future, it does point us toward a long-held belief of the Christian faith that God's covenant has a point toward which it is moving. That point is the consummation of all creation in a new heaven and a new earth. This hope is one that has shaped the vision of God's people for ages as they've understood that part of their response to God's covenantal call is to work in ways that make possible the vision of creation and all humanity participating in God's new creation. Of course this is not something done by our own efforts, but something that is accomplished as we respond to God's call to live in covenant and work in the power of God's Spirit, who empowers people in all times and places to live faithful lives in whatever situation we may find ourselves.

This witness to the covenantal character of God suggests two things. First, God is one who seeks to live in a covenant relationship with all creation, including humanity. Second, the covenant that God calls creation into is based on certain stipulations for humans and requires a response. We are called to be a set-apart people who work for *shalom* in this world. All people are called into this covenant; there are no exceptions. This is what we call the general calling. We are all called to live in covenant with God and seek to accomplish God's purpose of *shalom* in the world. However, it is also the case that certain ones are called to specific or missional callings in which they have particular work within the people of God as they help fulfill the covenant. It is important, though, to recognize that, according to the witness of Scripture, there is no single type of person who may be called in one of these two ways.

God Calls All Types of People for Covenantal Purposes

God calls people in all stages and places in life to fulfill missional and specific callings for the purposes of the covenant in this world. A simple survey of Scripture will note that God calls women and men, insiders and people on the margins, old, middle-aged, and young to live into the covenant and work for God's purposes.

God calls Abraham and Sarah late in life to go to a new land and become the parents of the promise people. Joseph is one of the youngest sons of Jacob, yet God uses him to deliver his family and surrounding nations from disaster. Moses is a criminal who doesn't believe he can do anything, but God calls him to lead Israel from slavery in Egypt to the edge of the Promised Land. God works through Deborah and Jael, two female military heroes, to help deliver Israel from oppression. Samuel is a young boy when God calls his name in a time when God's voice is faint. Saul is not the stateliest of his father's sons, but God chooses him to be the first king of Israel. Huldah is a prophetess who speaks God's message to Josiah, a king who begins to reign at age eight, so that a Torah revival begins in Jerusalem. Amos is a shepherd, and God calls him to go and prophesy to Samaria. Ezekiel is a prophet priest who is displaced from his homeland and experiences a serious trauma, yet he is able to offer words that call Israel back to the covenant at an important time in their journey.

Each of these Old Testament figures has a particular calling from God. Each one responds and helps the community of faith fulfill the covenant in a way that is contextually appropriate and vital for the people of God to be faithful in their time.

In the New Testament, Jesus calls and welcomes children, women, and men from all walks of life in ancient Judea. He welcomes children to come to him and explains that they understand something important about his mission. Women, such as Mary and Martha, Mary Magdalene, and the Samaritan woman at the well not only accompany Jesus but also participate in his work, proclaiming that God's kingdom is breaking in on the world. He calls disciples from all walks of life—zealots, soldiers, tax collectors, the unemployed, and fishermen. These disciples later become preachers, early church leaders, and missionaries. There are people like Paul, a Pharisee and religious teacher, who changes course mid-life to begin a new course as a bivocational missionary and tentmaker. Later followers of the Jesus movement include women such as Lydia, who in Acts 16 aids the work of God in Thyatira; Chloe, who leads a house church in Corinth; and Euodia and Syntyche, who work with Paul to spread the gospel in Philippi. There are young people like Timothy, whom Paul admonishes to not let anyone look down upon because of his youth.

All of Scripture witnesses that there is no one type of person God calls into covenant and no single point in life in which God may call you to serve in a specific or missional way.

God Calls Certain People to Specific or Missional Covenant Fulfillment

In Scripture, God calls some people to fill particular roles in order to help the community of faith fulfill the covenant. These people give their livelihood to shaping the people of God so they can work for *shalom*. In the Old Testament, three particular roles are important for thinking about leading God's people—prophet, priest, and shepherd. In the New Testament, a number of roles are mentioned, but few are explicitly defined. It is important to recognize that the early followers of Jesus begin to structure the way the community of faith is organized so they can work to accomplish the covenant.

In the ancient world, prophets are people called of God to live between the divine and human realms. Their calling is to a specific ministry that enables proper communication between the realms, ensuring the covenant continues. The prophets of Israel often deliver messages to call the people back to covenant faithfulness when they have strayed. At other times, they remind the people to trust in God's faithfulness to the covenant by offering words of hope. Prophets are often looked upon as persons of great spiritual insight, but often they walk a lonely journey because their words challenge the status quo and brokenness of the community. Today, we might think of prophets as people who are called to ministries that work at challenging structural injustice. One example of this could be someone whose vocation is as a social worker, ministering among the marginalized as a way of caring for those who are often overlooked. This type of missional calling is a way of ministering in an important area as the community of faith continues to work for *shalom.*

Priests in the ancient world are people who have been set aside to perform religious duties in the temple for the community of faith. In this world, much of the religious activity takes place in the temple or at a religious shrine. Priests offer sacrifices, pray, compose sacred texts, and lead the people in worship. The priests help people connect their everyday lives to the divine by taking common objects such as grain, oil, water, and blood and turning them into a means by which the people can connect with God. They also help people learn the correct ways of following God by scribing and teaching sacred texts. Sometimes, priests also function as judges, adjudicating particularly important cases between the people. In all of this, the priests serve an important role in helping the people fulfill the covenant. Today, we often think of ordained clergy, or those with a specific call, as priests. However, it might also be true that there are some missional ministries that fit this image too. It is important to think of the roles that a priest fulfills and think how a missional calling might still help the people of God fulfill the covenant.

Finally, the Old Testament image of a shepherd carries significant weight. Throughout Scripture the image of shepherd is one of comfort and care. The Lord is referred to as a shepherd in the Twenty-third Psalm and is said to comfort and protect the psalmist, even in the valley of the shadow of death. In the gospel of John, Jesus refers to himself as the "good shepherd" who lays down his life for his friends. There is good reason that this image carries such powerful connotations for the writers of Scripture. In the ancient world, the image is immediately meaningful because shepherding is part of their daily livelihood and practice. However, in addition to the imagery of care and protection for animals that the image awakens, the shepherd is also a symbol for the king in the ancient world. This second connotation is why Ezekiel 34 has an oracle about bad shepherds who lead the people astray.

The image of a shepherd as king may not seem likely for ministry, especially given some of the abuses of power that have occurred in some contexts; however, given that part of the original covenant that God makes with humanity includes language of kingly care, it might be worth noting that Israel's kings are supposed to be shepherds to their people. In fact, the law of the king in Deuteronomy 17 suggests that part of the primary responsibility of the king is to rightly interpret the Torah and lead the people in the ways of God. The image of shepherd then becomes one of not only care and protection of the people of God but also one of guidance in understanding God's covenant. Thus, when one thinks about either a specific or missional call to ministry, the image of a shepherd might be a helpful metaphor for thinking about how one goes about fulfilling that call.

In the New Testament, Jesus calls the disciples to come and follow him, and then he sends them out to do works of mercy and proclaim the words of the reign of God breaking forth. After Jesus's death and resurrection, the disciples lead the early movement that becomes the church. They are the ones who help form the people of God to continue the work of Jesus on earth as the daily work of meeting people's physical needs as well as proclaiming news of a spiritual revolution.

The following of Jesus expands beyond the point where the disciples can continue to lead it on their own. As the movement grows, more people must help in the leading of the ministry. Paul, in his writing to some of the early communities, discusses how God has called and empowered some to take up the vocation of leading the people of God. In his writing to the people of Corinth, Paul speaks of a number of gifts God has given for the common good. In 1 Corinthians 12, Paul says that some are apostles and some teachers, some have wisdom, and others have the gift of prophecy. These gifts are given by God to build up the community and help in the accomplishing of the work of God in love. The early followers of Jesus recognize that, though all people are called into covenant, certain people are gifted and further called to help shape and lead the community in accomplishing God's redemptive work.

However, not every person's calling and gifting looks the same. Paul is a missionary, a church planter, and a tentmaker who also writes letters from prison. Aquila and Priscilla are leather workers who also lead a local group of Jesus followers. Phoebe, who is mentioned in Romans 16:1, is called "a deacon of the church in Cenchreae." Though it is difficult to know exactly what the role of deacon is in that time, it is clear that her leadership is important to Paul as well as to her church. In the epistles to Timothy and Titus, the role of bishop is mentioned as another type of leader in the church. These various labels simply point to the fact that not every role is exactly the same. Though we have some defined ways of living into vocational ministry today, namely as pastors, missionaries, and educators, these are not the only ways God may call a person to a life of vocational ministry. Scripture witnesses that God calls a variety of people to work in a variety of ways to help the people of God fulfill the covenant. Whether it is a specific call to ordained ministry or a missional call, God is looking for people who are willing to respond with their gifts and passions to help the community of faith fulfill the covenant.

Where Do We Go from Here?

If Scripture witnesses to the above issues, then what should we do? Three things are important to remember.

First, we should remember that everyone is called into a covenantal relationship with God. God calls all of us to live into a reality that transforms us into a particular kind of people. As that particular kind of people, we work for God's overarching purpose of redemption in this world, a purpose that can be understood as *shalom*. This is the general calling on everyone's life. That said, there is a clear witness in Scripture that the community of faith has always needed people who are willing to be set aside for vocational leadership, people whose gifting, training, and purpose is to help guide and shape the community for fulfilling the covenant in its particular context.

Second, we should recognize that God is willing to work with anyone who will respond to the call to covenant. It is unfortunate that, in some places and times throughout history, there have been some limitations placed on certain groups and particular individuals as they have tried to respond to God's call. Scripture, however, witnesses to the fact that God calls and works with such a broad variety of people that we should be careful in telling anyone that God is not calling them to vocational ministry.

Finally, Scripture witnesses that this calling to vocational ministry may not look exactly the same for every person in every place and time in their life. There are many ways that people who are called may lift up and lead the community of faith in vocational ministry. Scripture witnesses to the fact that there is not one, singular picture of what vocational ministry looks like. Some may have a specific calling to ordained ministry. Others, however, may have a missional calling to a ministry that works to help the community of faith fulfill the covenant.

As you read the following narratives, take note of how God has called a variety of people into the covenant in a variety of ways. Notice how these different people have responded to that call in their particular contexts at different points in their lives. See how their responses are lived out in significant and unique ways in order to help shape the people of God so they can fulfill the covenant purposes of bringing about *shalom* in the world.

Then ask yourself, *What is my calling?* Perhaps God is calling you to vocational ministry. The witness of Scripture assures us that God still calls people to unique ministry opportunities. The question remains, *How will we respond to God's call?*

Discussion Questions

1. What does Scripture's witness to God's covenantal nature mean for the world and for your life?

2. In what ways do you see God working for *shalom* in your particular context?

3. If God can call people at any age or stage in life, what might that mean for your own life with regard to the possibility of God calling you to ministry?

4. Have you ever thought God might be calling you either to a specific or missional form of ministry?

5. To which image or images of ministry from Scripture's witness are you drawn?

Resources for Further Reading

Dozeman, Thomas B. *Holiness and Ministry*. New York: Oxford University Press, 2008.

Kysar, Robert. *Called to Care: Biblical Images of Social Ministry*. Minneapolis: Augsburg Fortress, 1991.

Olson, Laura R., Sue E. S. Crawford, and Melissa M. Deckman. *Women with a Mission: Religion, Gender, and the Politics of Women Clergy*. Tuscaloosa: University of Alabama Press, 2005.

Placher, William C., Editor. *Callings: Twenty Centuries of Christian Wisdom on Vocation*. Grand Rapids: Eerdmans, 2005.

Schuurman, Douglas J. *Vocation: Discerning Our Callings in Life*. Grand Rapids: Eerdmans, 2004.

Emerging Leader Narratives

Emerging leaders consist of young adults who are called to serve in full-time ministry and who are in the beginning stages of their ministry. These emerging leaders are becoming more visible and prominent in their prospective ministries. Some have already completed their theological education; others are still in the process of completing it. As they emerge into more established leaders in the church, they model for us a deep passion and desire to see the church and the kingdom of God advance. As you read the stories of their various calls to ministry, we trust you will catch a glimpse of their love for and commitment to God and the church.

Rev. Phillip Antilla
Senior Pastor
Ashland First United Methodist Church
Ashland, Oregon

I started serving God for all the wrong reasons. I did not grow up in an overly religious family, but I did grow up outside Atlanta, where it was a cultural norm to attend weekly church services. I wore a bowtie to church, and we had a potluck every Sunday.

When I was a bit older, we moved across the country and could not find a church that felt familiar to us, so we eventually stopped attending church altogether. As an extremely shy child, the break from church obligations was a huge relief to me. In time, my family and I shifted to nominal Christianity without making much effort to live out our faith.

As a teenager, I had no idea what to do with my life. A career aptitude test said I should consider becoming a bartender. I can only assume this was because I have a gift for talking to people—as long as there's some sort of physical distance between us. I figured perhaps I would become a schoolteacher or a writer. But what would I teach? What would I write? I felt like I was close to understanding what I was supposed to do with my life, but I could not see the whole picture. There was a veil over my eyes.

In high school, I was invited to attend a friend's church youth group. I was surprised to see other people like me having so much fun. I didn't have many friends, and, despite my introverted tendencies, this group appealed to me. I liked the games they played. I enjoyed the teaching. The youth pastor was nice. But most of all, I liked the music. It seemed like the people in the praise band had it all: They were popular, talented, and—apparently—good Christians. I decided my calling was to become one of these musicians. So I set out to learn how to play the guitar, confident this skill would help me become a good, popular Christian.

When I was seventeen, my church asked for volunteers to lead music at a middle school winter retreat. I immediately jumped at the opportunity. (If your goal is to feel cool or popular, try playing electric guitar at a middle school event. You'll get treated like a rock star.) I made sure I was fully prepared for the retreat. I packed hair gel, bandanas, and leather wrist bands—what more could one need for a weekend of spiritual formation? I was convinced it was going to be a great retreat. I remember all the Christian language I so carelessly used. I'm sure I said something like, "I'm praying for the Spirit to come to us," or, "I just want God to use me as a servant." But in truth, I didn't believe any of the buzz language I spouted. That weekend was all about *me*. It was *my* time to shine.

And guess what? The weekend was horrible.

I became ill not long after we arrived. I ran a fever and skipped staff meetings to stay in my cabin and sleep. Of course, I still managed to play in the band—because how could God work in the students' hearts without *me* (and my guitar)? But I remember finishing one song and turning to the band and saying, "That sounded horrible! Why did we play it in the key of F?"

The band members looked at me, puzzled, and said, "We were playing in G!"

Now, of course, I see what an excellent metaphor that incident was for my life at that time. I was playing the songs, but in the wrong key.

One disappointing evening during the retreat, I walked outside and turned to the skies and yelled, "God, how could you let me down like this? This was supposed to be a great weekend! People were going to be saved!"

Eventually I realized that, with a rising fever and pounding headache, I needed to get back to my cabin and my bed. I rushed back only to find a group of sixth-grade boys throwing snowballs inside! Everything was a mess. I yelled at them, telling them I felt horrible and they weren't helping. Then I told them to leave.

On their way out, one boy stopped in the doorway, looked at me, and said, "I hope you feel better soon. We'll pray for you." Then those boys proceeded to gather around the front porch of the cabin and, with no adult present, started to pray with a maturity beyond their years. One of the windows in the cabin was open, and as I lay in my bed, feverish, upset, and disappointed, I heard the prayers of those young boys, and their prayers changed my life.

One prayed, "God, we came here to be with Phil. We've been looking forward to this time with him. So please heal him. Make him healthy so he can be with us, so he can teach us and lead us."

My heart broke. That retreat's scriptural basis was 1 Corinthians 15:58: "Therefore, my beloved, be steadfast, immovable, always excelling in the work of the Lord, because you know that in the Lord your labor is not in vain" (NRSV).

We often say God must have a sense of humor, but I also think God understands the effect of well-placed sarcasm. It was as if God said to me, *Be not afraid! It's not as if your works have been done in vain! . . . Right?*

I realized *everything* I had done as a Christian had been in vain. I often said I was serving the Lord and God's people, but what a farce it was! Had I ever truly served another? Had I ever said to the Lord, "Here I am! Send me!"? I began to weep and pray. In that moment I offered my whole life to the Lord.

Almost instantly my fever seemed to disappear. My headache was gone. I stood up and walked outside as a new creation. John Wesley called this experience a new birth. I vividly remember that the snow was whiter and the air crisper than either ever had been before. The veil had been lifted, and I felt truly alive.

And as I stood on the front porch of that cabin, I heard the voice of the Lord simply say, *Do this*. It is just as clear to me now as it was then. I was called to lead others to new life.

I remember looking around the camp property, and the Spirit of God filled my imagination. I imagined young people hearing about Christ for the first time. I saw adults being faithful leaders. I saw families embodying what it looks like to be created in the image of God. I saw people's lives being radically changed by hearing and understanding the gospel in new and fresh ways.

Before that moment, I had no idea what I wanted to do for a career or vocation. But suddenly, it was like the only thing I had ever wanted to do was be a pastor. What's more, I didn't feel like I had to become someone else in order to live into that new calling. It was as if God had whispered to me: *Become who you are!*

I returned home to find that many of the avenues that first brought me into the Christian faith—though misused and misunderstood on my part—continued to be pathways to Christ and toward fulfilling my vocation. I went on a mission trip with the youth group and started to understand what it meant to truly serve God and the world. The youth pastor mentored me as a pastoral apprentice. My parents helped direct me to a Christian college in Idaho—Northwest Nazarene University, where I could study theology and Christian ministry. After graduating, I attended seminary and became an ordained minister. I now serve as a senior pastor. With each step in my journey, I've continued to live into the words from 1 Corinthians 15:58.

Sometimes I still wonder about the young boy who prayed for me. I don't remember his name, but he played such an important role in my life. The Bible speaks often about how anything can be accomplished by faith in prayer. I often wonder if the most honest prayer I've ever heard was from that boy. Did he really want me to be healed? Did he really want me to be a teacher? A leader? I may never know for certain, but I *am* sure the Spirit of God worked in my life that day. It is no coincidence that on the day I became aware of my pastoral calling, someone else did their part and called on my behalf.

Rev. Nick Bollinger
Owner
Junction Coffee
Oklahoma City, Oklahoma

Callings are interesting things. Even the way we speak of them is somewhat peculiar—as if they are symbolic objects bestowed upon us from the great beyond that solidify our destinies forever. In my mind, there is a sense that, when we talk about a calling to ministry, we paint a picture similar to the sorting hat from Hogwarts in the *Harry Potter* series: A group of people sit in a room waiting anxiously to hear on what trajectory they will be launched that will undoubtedly shape the rest of their lives and the lives of generations to come.

"Missionary!" the hat yells out as everyone cheers.

"Children's pastor!"

"Youth leader!"

"Church planter!"

But callings, like everything else in the real world, don't work like that—or at least, it didn't work like that for me. I do know people who claim they've always known they were called to specific ministry, but that's not me.

I come from a family that believes there are only two things in the world that are constant: One is that God loves you more than you could ever fathom, and two is change. So I grew up with an understanding that God will always love me and all the people of the world and that nothing will stay the same forever. Obviously there are implications that accompany that line of thought, some of which can become problematic if we follow them too far. But it was less what my parents said and more the testimony of their lives that shaped this philosophy in our household. My dad, who has only been a Christian as long as he's been alive, has had six jobs in four completely different industries, and currently is working on a seventh job

41

in a fifth industry. My mother has had seven jobs, including mother-hood, in three different industries. She is also working on her next move. When I was eight, we moved from California to Denver, and I had four grandparents. When I graduated from high school I only had two, and by the time I graduated from college, all of them had passed away. These instances were, unfortunately, only a small part of my experiences with death as an adolescent; that experience also included young children, classmates, and friends.

Nothing stays the same forever. But this sort of chaotic, uncertain future that I have come to see as a beautiful element of the divine character is, perhaps, what my entire call to ministry hinges upon.

When I was fourteen my dad, at that time an executive pastor at a Nazarene congregation in the Denver area, went to Ethiopia on a short-term mission trip. When he came home, my family spent several days listening to all the stories of how lives were changed and miracles happened. In my fourteen-year-old mind, this was the best epic I had ever heard! And so, when the storytelling was finished I told my dad, "The next time you go, I want to go with you." We went the following year.

Anyone who goes to Africa, no matter their age, will tell you it messes with the way you see the world. So imagine how upside down things got for me. I was fifteen, had been born into the white middle class, attended a nice school, and had a nice life—all of which was suddenly juxtaposed with the poverty of Ethiopia.

I remember distinctly that, toward the end of the trip, we decided as a group to purchase water bottles for everyone on the project site where we were working. They had been collecting our empties all week, using them to carry dirty, unsafe water for their families. One woman's face is burned into my memory. When she received her full bottle of clean water, she smiled from ear to ear and pressed the bottle to her chest as if she had found a lost and beloved child. I knew at that moment that I wanted to be in the business of sharing hope and love.

Over the next year, I wrestled with what this calling meant and looked like in my life. It was my junior year of high school—an appropriate time, I suppose, to be having this somewhat existential crisis. The main problem was that I didn't want to be a pastor—only because my dad was a pastor, and I wanted to blaze my own trail. But then my dad said something to me that changed everything. "You know, just because you're a pastor or missionary for a little while doesn't mean you'll be that forever. The important thing is that you're obedient to what God wants you to do *now*."

I did not want to say yes to a call to ministry and end up feeling stuck behind the same, boring pulpit somewhere on the other side of the world for the rest of my life. I wanted *adventure*. I wanted to do something no one else had done before. I wanted to be God's warrior, on the edge of the unknown, pushing the envelope, changing the world. And to me, being a pastor was the exact opposite of that dream.

I prayed and pondered and eventually settled on becoming a missionary. I went to Ethiopia again when I was seventeen to affirm my decision for myself, and then I enrolled at Southern Nazarene University as a theology ministry major with a missions minor. Halfway through my first missions class, I dropped the minor. I found out that missionaries tend to be trainers and administrators more so than trailblazers. Training and administration are important gifts and God-given skills, but that didn't feel like the right direction for me, at least not yet.

For the next four years I considered different ideas of what serving God might look like in a career sense. I interned with children and tried out senior pastor and college pastor roles with a satellite church. During this process, I intentionally avoided youth ministry. Then, between my junior and senior years at SNU, I went to Swaziland. (I promise God speaks to people who don't go to Africa!)

We were eating lunch after a hard, physical morning digging irrigation trenches for a community garden when an inebriated man came stumbling through our picnic. He greeted everyone in a friendly, drunken way and then plopped down right in the middle of our group. After a while I glanced at him. He was sort of hunched over and semi-lucid. Then, all of a sudden, he straightened up, looked straight into my eyes, and opened his hands. In that moment, though he didn't speak, I heard a voice say, *Look at me,* and my heart broke.

Look at me. See what I have become. See who I am. Know me and my misery. See me with your heart. See me with Jesus's eyes. Know me as Christ loves me. And show me that he cares.

This is my calling. Not to a ministry or to *the* ministry as a role or career, but a mission on my life to be the extension of God's love for other people. I followed that call through graduation to three years of youth pastoring in Oklahoma. But then, in the summer of 2013, my heart became burdened for those beyond my reach at that time. My church was isolated from the reality of this world, and I could not reach beyond that bubble. The work I was doing was good. In fact, I know that God radically transformed several lives in my ministry, but change had arrived at my doorstep once again.

I was called to start a coffee-shop ministry. My wife and I took a double-decker bus and converted it into a food truck. We serve food and coffee while building relationships and sharing the love of Jesus. It's a little crazy, but it has been awesome.

This story is filled with the personal pronoun "I" on purpose. Someone once passed on to me a paraphrase of an idea theologian Frederick Buechner is known for making famous: "Your calling is where your deepest passion intersects with the world's greatest need." For years, I was afraid of a calling. I was afraid that a calling would doom me to failure because I had nothing to do with the selection process. I was afraid that, eventually, my obedient, servant heart would burn out. I was afraid that being called meant some arbitrary assignment in God's mission where you are stuck peeling holy potatoes until you keel over dead.

But I've been learning instead that, like the sorting hat does with Harry Potter in his first year at Hogwarts, God takes our desires into consideration.

Saying yes to a call is embarking on a journey where you and God together discern how divine character can best be revealed through your gifts, talents, and passions. Sometimes, yes, that's being a children's pastor in Nowhere, Kansas. Or sometimes it's putting an espresso machine in a double-decker bus. And it may change over time, or it may not. Regardless of the specifics, God is still calling all of us to reveal God to the world. And saying yes to that call is simply saying yes to the journey—wherever it may take you.

Rev. Megan Krebs
Student
Nazarene Theological Seminary
Kansas City, Missouri

As I sat in her office, I avoided Dr. Diane Leclerc's eyes by staring at my feet. I was in the process of changing my major from ministry. I wanted anything that would help me graduate sooner and get into law school faster. All I needed to do was file the final paperwork.

It was the fall semester of my sophomore year at Northwest Nazarene University. Classes had been in session for a few weeks, and the year had already proven nearly unbearable. As a resident assistant (RA), I watched a young woman be overcome by drug addiction and eventually withdraw from school, even though we made every effort to help her. A few weeks later, the youngest son of a family I grew up with was killed during a hunting accident. It happened just a week before his eighth birthday. I felt jagged and cracked and ready to fall apart.

Dr. Leclerc apparently heard about my possible change of major. So one afternoon, while I was visiting the office of another professor in the department, she poked her head around the door of her office and crooked her finger at me. She said, "I've heard that you and I need to talk."

Stammering, I asked, "A-about what?"

She replied, "You're thinking about changing majors, but you need to come and talk to me first."

The next afternoon, I somehow bolstered enough courage to knock on her door. So there I sat, studying the cracks in my Converse, wondering how Dr. Leclerc had learned of my plans and wondering how I could quickly exit this conversation.

Dr. Leclerc said, "I don't understand why so many of you drop out of the ministry program, especially you young women. Didn't you expect it to be difficult?"

My eyes stayed on my shoes. How was I supposed to tell her that the past few weeks had been hell? That this decision had nothing to do with studying or training for ministry—those classes were one of the few places I actually felt at peace. The truth was that I was broken by loss and deeply depressed. As I looked around at my gifted classmates, I felt in my heart that I was not like them, so I concluded I could not possibly be a pastor. Instead, I was going to be a lawyer. I was either too stubborn to admit it, or possibly, I could not articulate it. So I stayed silent and shrugged at the floor.

Dr. Leclerc continued to stare at me. Then she sighed deeply and said, "Megan, I know lots of people would tell you not to do this, but I think there are certain circumstances in which it is appropriate to ask God for a sign. I think this is a big enough issue that you can ask."

"Okay," I said.

I had no intention of following through, but I have learned over the years that Dr. Leclerc has a way of smelling such deception, so she made me pray with her and talk with her a while longer. She talked about many things I had no interest in hearing.

After a while, I snapped. I said, "Why can't anyone just accept that this is what's right for me? Even my parents, who have never supported me going into ministry in the first place, are against me! The first words out of my mom's mouth were, 'Couldn't you do both? Why do you have to stop being a pastor?' My dad told me I was wrong and that I'm supposed to be a pastor. But when I was in high school, it was a battle to get them to support me studying ministry. Last weekend, when I visited my aunt in Carson City, she introduced me to every one of her friends as her 'niece who is going to be a pastor!' Why can't you all just let me go?"

Dr. Leclerc blinked and gave me a look I've come to anticipate over the years. She said, "Megan, your family has suddenly started supporting your call after never doing so before, and you don't think that's a sign? You don't think that maybe, just maybe, God is trying to speak to you through them?"

Silence.

Dr. Leclerc said, "I can't force you to follow it, but let me say that you will never be at peace if you run from this calling."

I shrugged again and soon found a reasonable excuse to leave her office. As I wandered across the NNU campus back to my dorm, my feet took the scenic route. My mind would not stop running the tape of our conversation. I thought back to the first time I felt the call of God to go into ministry.

I was at Northwest District Nazarene church camp for the first time, about to begin my freshman year of high school, and the preacher spoke about the difference between asking God where the line that defines sin lies and asking God how to be holy. He described the difference between dead religion and living in Christ as the difference between wanting to know the exact parameters of sin and throwing all of yourself into following the life of Jesus. That evening, during an altar call, I watched students flood forward.

Youth pastors lined the walls. As students moved forward, the appropriate pastors got up and went to their teens. They prayed with their students, hugged them, and led them out of the chapel when they were ready. It was the beautiful meeting between the broken and the called. It was like watching the kingdom of God take root in that place.

God lit a fire in my heart as I watched these various scenes repeat themselves in that camp chapel. In that moment, I knew I was being called to ministry. When I told Darin, my own youth pastor, about my call, I felt like I was voicing something powerful and earth shattering, and Darin celebrated with me.

Since that first call, I had never doubted whether God was calling me to ministry. So why was I doubting now? I stuffed my hands into my pockets as I meandered around campus, my brow furrowed with distress. As my walk grew longer and longer, I thought about Darin's discipleship of me through high school. He and his wife, Sabrina, took me under their wing and mentored me through those crucial years.

I thought about all the ways in which God had led me in this call. My mind kept landing on what Darin said to me just before I left for NNU. It seemed that Dr. Leclerc's words just a few moments ago were an echo of Darin's affirmation: "If you can do anything besides ministry without it affecting your relationship with God, do it. Ministry is a difficult and heartbreaking road. But, if God has called you to ministry, it will be the very best thing you could ever hope for, and it is the only thing that will bring you peace."

This peace I kept hearing about was what I desperately needed in my life. And not peace as a mere lack of conflict, but peace as *shalom*—the abiding wholeness and wellness that all of creation longs for and that only God can create. I prayed that day for clarity. I prayed to know what would bring me *shalom*.

Eventually, my meanderings led me back to my dorm room. As I sat down on my bed, I looked down at the form I had filled out for a change of major. The black ink on the white paper hardly seemed to communicate the gravity of what I was considering. I sat and prayed with that page in my lap. When I finished, I folded the form and placed it in my desk drawer. Quickly, I shot an email to the registrar's office asking them to discard my paperwork for the transfer of majors.

I expected an immediate peace to overwhelm me like a wave, but instead it felt more like intentionally stepping out into a warm rain. At first, it was uncomfortable, but soon it felt soothing and familiar—as much a part of me as my own skin. God's voice was indeed small and quiet, but it never stopped speaking. I just had to learn to listen through the rain.

Rev. Cassandra Lara
Education Coordinator
Mother's Refuge
Independence, Missouri

It's nothing new to use the metaphor of a journey to understand our lives. But a teacher once elaborated on the timeless analogy, explaining that every single experience alters one's journey. It may only be by a degree or two, but years down the road, that small degree will have led to an entirely different location than another one would have.

The summer after my freshman year of college, I worked at a camp in Colorado. In our first staff chapel service, I felt a weight on my chest. I had trouble concentrating on the service, but I remember the speaker preaching about Peter stepping out of the boat to Jesus. He challenged us to evaluate where we found ourselves in the story. Were we the people on the beach, too afraid to leave shore? Were we still in the storm, lost in fear? Or were we Peter, jumping out to Jesus in blind faith, not knowing what came next? In that service, I surrendered to God. I admitted that I was willing to jump out of the boat—whatever that meant.

For the first time in my life I heard the clear voice of God in my head—missions, in Africa. Before that, my plan for life was boring, but at least I had decided: I wanted to be a high school history teacher who wore ugly sweaters but was still liked and respected. A mission call to Africa presented a 180-degree change, so naturally, I freaked out. I struggled the majority of the summer with what a call to missions meant for me. I prayed for peace almost every day, and in a simple conversation with a friend at our camp's archery range, I suddenly realized I was not scared anymore.

In August, a couple days before my sophomore year was to start, I walked into Northwest Nazarene University's religion department and told them I needed to change my major. While I still was not certain how all this was going to work out, I began settling into my new plan, which led me to studying abroad in Uganda. There were several fraction-of-a-degree turns that semester. I certainly did not return to the States the same person I was when I left. In witnessing extreme poverty and the greedy, overt injustices of economics and politics, I struggled to understand God's love and participation in the world. Those I met in Uganda did not seem to share my doubts, though. I survived by remembering their faith and their strong emphasis on communal presence.

Early in my missions major study, I recognized my passion for social justice and compassionate ministries. Evangelism is essential, to be sure, but that was not where I felt called. I figured that if someone is hungry or cold, they are not going to care much for what I have to say about faith and salvation. Instead, I wanted to address the whole person. I wanted to be a voice for the voiceless, for the forgotten, and for those on the fringe of society. I envisioned myself more as a bridge than a shepherd. I wanted to connect church people with the surrounding community.

My experiences in Uganda only affirmed my call. In fact, my entire theology of God's love developed a deep understanding of the importance of being present with others, wherever they may be. I still really did not know how that was going to work out in the real world of a paying job, but I had faith and hope that I would live out my call of missions by being present—whatever and wherever that meant.

The need for a final internship to graduate led me overseas again. Obviously, with a missions degree, I assumed I would become a traditional missionary, so the more experience I gained beforehand, the better, right? I worked for ten months in Bulgaria with a wonderful Nazarene missionary family and shifted another degree in my journey. Through the wisdom of another missionary's experience, I learned that *a* call from God does not have to be the *final* call. It well could be, but it also may simply be a call for right now, or for the next step. That revelation freed me from my burden surrounding what I felt was my initial and very specific call to missions. Therefore, I was not disobedient if I followed a new direction, a less traditional path from typical, overseas-missionary journeys.

I returned to the United States with my newfound freedom and began my education at Nazarene Theological Seminary (NTS) in Kansas City, continuing my pursuit of ordination. I have great appreciation and gratitude for all the education I have received in my undergraduate and graduate studies. I am who I am because of the people I've met and the lessons I've learned along the way. While my educational degrees have not necessarily pegged me into a specific job, they have certainly grounded me in why I do what I do. My calling is to serve God's mission in the world, and I obey that calling by being present with those in need.

After I graduated from NTS, I continued to serve in the church while also working multiple jobs to make ends meet, and all of these little fractions of turns led me to a completely different place than I ever imagined. Through the crucible and fire, I emerged stronger. I blame no one, but after a couple of years trying to fit in what felt like a cookie-cutter concept of ministry, I peacefully quit my pursuit of ordination and left the church I currently attended. Once again, I surrendered what I had created as *my* plans, for *my* concept of merging *my* passions with what I thought *I* was supposed to do—a struggle that nearly broke me. I finally let go of my own preconception of what being *called* meant. Missions are anywhere and everywhere. I learned that my call was not tied to what I do but, rather, to who I am to be.

In my final internship for my graduate studies, I began to work at Mother's Refuge, a nonprofit homeless shelter for pregnant and parenting teens. Mother's Refuge provides housing for pregnant and parenting women between the ages of twelve and twenty-one. They can come at any point in their pregnancies and stay through their children's first year of life. Obstacles for these young women include but are not limited to past abuses of alcohol and drugs, past traumas of sexual, physical, and emotional abuse, being single mothers with little to no emotional or financial support, and having no safe, stable environment in which to live.

My role at Mother's Refuge has evolved over the years from house parent to education coordinator, but here I finally feel the connection between my call and my passion. I am present with those forgotten by society. I try to be a voice to those who are neglected and ignored. I still long to be a bridge between the world of church and the world of other—worlds that often seem vastly distant from each other—but I'm continually relearning to trust God with each step.

I do not know how long I will be in this context or where my next step will lead. God may call me back to a traditional ministry role or to an entirely new field. I do not know, and most days, I am content. In any ministry, there are many rough days with few thank-you notes. I have been yelled at and threatened. I have nearly burned myself out by taking on too much and neglecting personal care. But there are also bright, peaceful days, and there are positive relationships. I have been later hugged by those who have yelled. I enjoy inside jokes and real conversations with the staff and residents. Most of our young women are still teenagers, and with that reality comes both torture and joy. They struggle with themselves and with rules, and I am grateful to be part of their lives as they learn to become mature adults and responsible mothers. I may never see how some of these young women are affected in the long run, but I pray they are better for having been through our program and ministry. I also pray they realize that everything we do for them is done out of love—out of a real, true call from God.

Rev. Jenna Redmond Stout
Candidate Development Coordinator
Nazarene Global Missions, Global Ministry Center
Lenexa, Kansas

Vermilion was the color of the carpet, the pews, the altars—seemingly even the walls—of the small Nazarene church I called home throughout my growing-up years. Brick and dark wood complemented the red—obvious marks of a church whose decorators hailed from a decade past. It was on that rust-red carpet that my seven-year-old self knelt, surrounded by both biological and church family, as we prayed for two missionaries who would soon depart for Romania. The missionary service that evening was typical. Services of this sort were a once-a-month occurrence, sandwiched between Sunday evenings dedicated to testimony sharing and Singspirations.

As a child, I loved Sunday evening services. I loved the sharing of stories and the informal atmosphere. I loved the praise choruses and the freedom to sit with friends. But most of all, I loved to hear the missionaries speak. We hosted missionaries a few times a year—individuals for whom we regularly prayed and whose pictures decorated our LINKS bulletin board. Their stories captivated me. Even as a child, I was sensitive to God moving in the hearts of people and inviting them to participate in God's mission around the world.

But this particular service was different. My parents have told the story so many times it is hard to distinguish my true memories. It was a sacred moment as people gathered around the missionaries whose words had stirred something in my spirit, words I feel deeply even today. In the final moments of the service, we gathered at the altar to lay hands on and pray aloud for the women who were faithfully following the call of God. During the open prayer time, I felt compelled to speak. With true childlike simplicity, I acknowledged the call to ministry God was already impressing upon my life. In the company of those who would continue to play a prominent role in raising me, I put into words the inner stirrings of my young heart. I answered out loud the invitation God had extended to me. "I want to serve you as a missionary when I grow up."

What did this statement mean? As a child and teenager, I had a pretty good idea of what it meant to be a missionary woman. A missionary woman lived overseas. A missionary woman was a pastor or married to a pastor. A missionary woman wore long dresses and drab blouses. A missionary woman should be proficient in foreign languages and be generally nice. Pursuing my call to missions meant I needed to abstain from anything that went against the Ten Commandments. I should not date boys who did not also profess a strong call to ministry (eliminating any chance of a date in high school), and it was imperative that I participate in Bible quizzing and read every missionary book published by the Church of the Nazarene.

When I was fifteen, shortly after Nazarene Youth Congress (now Conference) in 2003, God spoke again. In the quiet, morning hours of an ordinary Saturday, God spoke to my heart and confirmed the call that had been placed there years earlier: *I am calling you to be my missionary.* I went about my day charged with emotion but unable to put the experience into words. In the afternoon I sat with my mom and shared the childhood call of which God had so vividly reminded me. Even now it is difficult to describe the significance of those early-morning hours—not only the thickness of God's presence but also the weightiness of accepting the call to serve.

Not long after that Saturday morning, I went on my first short-term, cross-cultural mission trip. This would be the first of many opportunities God has provided for me to serve in different countries. Although each of these experiences has brought its own unique offering, the summer I spent in Mumbai, India, stands out as the most significant in the development of my call. I traveled to Mumbai in 2007 at the age of nineteen. During the eight weeks I spent there, I needed to rely on God's strength in a more tangible way than I ever had. Such utter dependence developed my faith, inspired conviction, and solidified my call to serve.

While attending Northwest Nazarene University, God gave me the opportunity to explore my call in a new context. How would my childhood longing hold up in academia? Amid the piles of books, campus events, and vigorous internships, God met me. God continued to speak into and affirm the call on my life. My classes invited me to think critically about missions, to observe the trends and shifting paradigms, and to think practically about cross-cultural ministry in the twenty-first century.

During these formative years at college, a tension began to grow in me. What if missions did not look the way I once thought it did? What if I had misunderstood or misinterpreted God's call? I began to wonder if missionaries *must* be pastors, doctors, or teachers in outdated clothes. It seemed to me that God was using accountants, athletic coaches, photographers, and baristas to advance the kingdom. Could this be right?

In 2010, I married my husband. He studies music, reads classic literature, and is perhaps the most loyal of all Denver sports fans. He is not a pastor (my twelve-year-old self would be shocked). However, his faithfulness to the call God has put on his life has been a testimony in my own life. Together, we have followed God's leading and served in a variety of contexts from local church ministry in Idaho, to church planting in rural New Zealand, to community building in a suburban Kansas coffee shop, to teaching English in urban Korea. Our first few years of marriage have been full of rich experiences, beautiful relationships, and important growth.

Today, God calls me to serve Christ and his church by mobilizing others for cross-cultural ministry. I have the opportunity to develop and deploy volunteer missionaries for the Church of the Nazarene. I never would have dreamed that I would serve God in this way, but

God continues to show me that *calling* is much broader and richer than I can understand or imagine.

Over the past few years, God has been teaching me that my childhood expectations for missions and ministry didn't do justice to God's plan. For me, fulfilling God's call to cross-cultural ministry has looked more like coffee time with young moms and grammar lessons with Korean elementary students than it has the exotic tales told in the missionary books that captivated me as a child. For my husband and me, fulfilling God's call to cross-cultural ministry has looked like Friday night dinners with our Korean coworkers, intentional times of building relationships around the table. It has looked like Moms' Night Out and preschool music clubs in New Zealand, despite not having children of our own. It has looked like weekly Bible classes in a public school, baking lessons with a friendly barista, and riding motorbikes with junior high boys in muddy fields during school holidays. Over and over, God has provided opportunities for me to share the love of Christ in cross-cultural settings. But it hasn't looked the way I once imagined it would.

Fulfilling my call today looks mostly like a desk job. I sit in a cubicle writing emails and attending meetings. But there is great fulfillment in spending my days investing in those to whom God has called me for this season—men and women who desire to fulfill God's call on *their* lives in cross-cultural ministry.

Coincidentally, a familiar shade of carpet adorns the sanctuary of the Nazarene church I currently attend, some two thousand miles away from home. Recently, the red carpet jogged my memory, and I was reminded of the occasion when I first felt God's call. The magnitude of that moment more than twenty years ago awed me. What kind of God speaks to the heart of a seven-year-old? Who am I, that God invites *me* to participate in God's mission?

The patience and faithfulness of God are constant themes in my life. God is ever so patient with the little-girl-turned-woman who is slow to catch on to the bigness of the call. God challenges my worldview, grows my perspective, and re-educates me in what it means to follow God's call and participate in cross-cultural ministry. Likewise, God has been faithful. Along the way, there have been questions—not so much, *Am I called?* but, rather, *Am I enough?*

The resounding answer in these moments is always, *You are not enough. I* AM *enough.*

The God who spoke to the heart of the little girl in the little church with the outdated carpet about the big things she would be asked to participate in someday is the God who continues to call us and invite us to participate in what God is already doing around the world. It is our privilege to answer this call.

Rev. Krystal Wigginton
Youth Pastor
Garden Grove Church of the Nazarene
Garden Grove, California

I am a third-generation Nazarene on both sides of my family. If I had not been born on a Saturday night, I would have been at church the first Sunday after my birth. I grew up in the church, and every member of my extended family has been an active participant in the happenings of the church.

I started my faith journey when I was four years old, sitting in a Sunday school class taught by my grandmother. She showed a picture of Jesus and talked about the relationship she had with him. To a four-year-old, it sounded like the best friend you could ever want, so I signed up. This decision led to years of highs and lows in my walk with God, and many come-to-Jesus camp experiences at the altar.

Then I began high school. My mother was part of our district's Nazarene Missions International (NMI) council, which meant she dragged me to all the NMI events. It was exciting to meet missionaries and hear their stories about how they depended on God. I wanted to learn dependence on God. When I was sixteen, I had a feeling in the pit of my stomach that God wanted me to be a missionary. I chalked it up to hanging out with too many missionaries, but the nagging never went away.

When I was seventeen, I attended Nazarene Youth Conference (NYC), an event designed for Nazarene high school students to gather together, draw close to God, meet interesting people, serve the community, and have some fun. I had seen two of my three older siblings experience NYC and witnessed their faith radically change. I wanted that experience for myself, so I went to NYC. By the last night I was feeling rejected by God because this supposedly amazing experience had yet to happen. There was only one service left, and so far, the speaker for the week had done nothing but bore me to tears. I woke up the last morning with a feeling that the final service would be different and that I needed to pay attention. So I did, and I was not disappointed. The speaker talked about following God's calling in your life no matter what that call looked like. That word was exactly what I needed to hear.

At the close of the service the speaker asked anyone who felt God calling them to some type of Christian service to come forward. I heard an audible voice say, *Go* in my ear, so I went. I crawled over armrests to get to the center aisle and moved across the stadium floor to get as close to the platform as I could. I knelt on the ground with my head on the floor. In that moment, I not only told God I would go wherever, but I also surrendered my life to God and chose to follow God's will for my life.

Then there was a young man I thought God had made just for me. He was the son of a former missionary who had become a pastor. He was born on the mission field. If anyone would understand a prodding to missions, he should. However, his beliefs were a little different than mine, and it took me longer than I'd like to admit to realize I could not live with the differences. (When you feel God calling you to something, and the person in whom you are romantically interested stands in the way, that person is definitely not the one for you!) This young man did not think women should be in positions of authority over men. At first I thought he meant as pastors, and I figured I could live with that because I don't like being the center of attention and didn't really plan to be a pastor. I figured I could still fulfill my calling by serving the church like the women of my family had done for generations. It took me two and a half years to understand that he did not even think my mother should be NMI president!

So the boyfriend had to go. It was a difficult decision to make. After the relationship ended, my grandmother flew me out of state to spend three months with her and my grandfather. This woman had several different versions of the Bible on her nightstand; she read through one, put it on the bottom of the stack, and moved on to the next. I do not know how many times she read through the Bible in each version, but she was well versed. It took me about a week living with my grandparents to realize my former boyfriend had turned me into someone I did not recognize. I had become everything he wanted me to become, rather than becoming who I am. God used my grandmother to help set me straight. During those three months, my grandmother gave me every book she had about faith and about becoming a person with an unquenchable fire for God.

It took almost every day of that three months for God to deconstruct who I had let myself turn into and put me back together the way God wanted me to be, and I knew the reconstructed rendering would be tested. Sure enough, when I got off the plane after returning home, my ex was there waiting. It took him only two days to realize I was a completely different person. I was grateful to God for making me noticeably different. I felt different on the inside and was glad the light was shining through on the outside.

That fall, I started attending a local university and getting more involved in leadership roles at church. Slowly God started guiding me toward being an educator, and I thought that was perfect because it could be done in this country! The path toward education was great until, one day, I was standing in my junior high Sunday school class and heard the same audible voice from that service at NYC saying, *Missions.*

I told God the same thing I had years prior: "I'll go wherever you send me."

Then I had a Gideon moment. I tested God by talking to the one person I knew was praying for me relentlessly, my biggest supporter, and the only person who would be blatantly honest—my mother. I waited a few months to allow time for prayer, but one night after we finished an NMI convention and headed to dinner, I simply told my mother that I felt God calling me to be a missionary. She burst into tears and said something I will never forget: "It's about time! God told me years ago!"

I completed degrees at Northwest Nazarene University and Nazarene Theological seminary to fulfill my educational requirements for ordination. There is no better time than when you're a college student or seminarian to learn how to depend on God for everything. There are times were I look back and wonder how I ever survived. There is a passage of Scripture that has rung true in my life over and over again, and which I often lived out while in school: "Do not fear, for I have redeemed you; I have summoned you by name; you are mine. When you pass through the waters, I will be with you; and when you pass through the rivers, they will not sweep over you. When you walk through the fire, you will not be burned; the flames will not set you ablaze. For I am the LORD your God, the Holy One of Israel, your Savior" (Isaiah 43:1b–3a).

I work bivocationally, and my fun job is serving as a youth pastor. Right now I am fulfilling my call to missions by helping our church engage in missional service to our community. I was recently ordained as an elder in the Church of the Nazarene and am looking into various PhD programs. I plan to continue fulfilling my call to missions by serving and teaching on the mission field one day. For now, however, being able to spend time with young people and show them how real God can be, how God cares about the little things, and nurturing in them the calls they feel on their own lives is something that brings me joy.

As I look back on my life, I realize there really are no memories in which the church is not somehow involved. Everything I have is from God. I am hard-pressed to find a better life worth living.

Established Leader Narratives

Established leaders are ministers who are established in their ministry calling and have been recognized by the church and their peers. These are well-respected leaders. They have journeyed in ministry for a number of years by overcoming challenges and embracing new opportunities. These leaders are women and men who mentor and disciple others to build the church and the kingdom of God. As you read the call of these established leaders, we hope you are reminded that the God who calls always remains faithful.

Rev. Gabriel J. Benjiman
Pastor and Africa Nazarene Regional Education Coordinator
Morningside Community Church of the Nazarene
Durban, South Africa

The word *calling* implies a voice. My personal experience of the call has not graced me with a loud, audible voice like the one in the Gospels that says, "This is my Son, whom I love; with him I am well pleased" (Matthew 3:17; 17:5; see also Mark 1:11; Luke 3:22; 2 Peter 1:17). My call was more like the whisper Elijah has to listen for in 1 Kings 19. The call as a whisper causes one to incline an ear. It forces one to lean forward and pay attention. Of course, most of those who are called would like to hear a loud, affirming voice or some manifestation of mountain-splitting wind or landscape-reorganizing earthquakes. I settled for the whisper. Cataclysmic calls are good for testimony, but whispers are great for relationships.

I encourage anyone who may believe that God is calling not to expect an audible voice to present the invitation to participate in the vocation of Christian service. Over the ages God's pattern of invitation and conversation is often a soft, almost silent whisper. In my life, the whisper has usually been in response to my questions: *Who am I? Why did you call me? What do you want me to do?* The call of God helps us to know his voice and follow his direction.

The Calling Is Designed around an Individual's Core Passions

Over nearly two and a half decades of having said yes to the ministry of service, I have found that education and experience have become part of the dialogue in the calling. The calling is an ongoing conversation between God and me. Early in my ministry I recognized that God called me based on who I was. I knew that, if nothing else, I was called to be a preacher and teacher. Others later confirmed what God saw in me. My passion has always been rhetoric and clear communication of the gospel, even if that meant dramatizing a Bible story while preaching.

Such individual design through culture and context is what God uses to touch the very people around us. These are external habits and cultural knowledge that become part of our behavior. Not only is God interested in shaping my external behavior, but he has also been at work spiritually, forming my internal beliefs. I grew up in a Hindu-African context, where belief in the supernatural is culturally entrenched. My current local context is of a Hindu-Islamic-African influence.

God uses our cultural and personal passions to communicate his love to redeem and correct the cultures and contexts from which we were saved. Isaiah recognizes his own deficiencies and his passions for his people in his calling (see Isaiah 6). He hears God ask, "Whom shall I send?" (v. 8) and responds because he is a man of passionate expressions of salvation for a people about whom he is passionate.

The Calling Is a Denial of our Controlling Preferences

In my response to the call of God, it was necessary to identify leaders who spoke the truth uncompromisingly. These spiritual leaders often advised me on next steps. Spiritual people in my life often confirmed later that the calling is first a call to salvation. In other words, God led me to become safe from self-destructive choices. Second, it was a call to be sanctified. In South Africa twenty-five years ago that meant having a defining moment of spiritual activity that set me apart for active service in the local church. There I served in every possible way, often executing humble tasks. Such is the nature of developing influence.

The call to salvation and sanctification is indeed a laying-down entirely of self. Jesus spoke of this call to follow as a denial of self and acceptance of a cross. This self-denial is about laying down one's personal preferences and priorities in order to fully submit to the terms of God's purposes. The *me I want to be* versus the *me God desires* must be exposed. This exposure creates the polarity that necessitates the denial of what I want in order to take up the cross God has in store—it's what I need to fully optimize God's purpose in my life. The cross is a denial of our own preferred outcomes. Out of necessity the cross calls us to say with Jesus, "Yet not my will, but yours be done" (Luke 22:42).

The Calling Requires Discernment of God's Continued Presence

God calls us to a journey with him. God's presence is not merely an assurance that he will bail us out of trouble, as though he only underwrites our potential deficits. While God's presence does include gracious intervention when we are unable to resource our service, it also bears upon the idea that God will remain a companion on the journey to those whom he calls. Being confident about the call is to be confident that God remains a companion even if he is silent for long periods of time.

In the Old and New Testaments, Moses, David, Jeremiah, Gideon, Mary, Andrew, Peter, and the rest of God's servants all have very different purposes to fulfill. Their callings, as related in the biblical narratives, tell us of God having a carefully orchestrated plan, and he helps his called ones avert the wicked plans of their antagonists. This seemingly clear pattern of God's activities unfolds in the story of the Exodus as God is seen miraculously controlling the environment around Moses. Reading the Exodus story in one sitting can inspire in the reader immediate hope of a very present God who is always active. But church people and Christian workers know that this is not always the case. It may take time to realize that God is always present in relationship because he is not always actively rubber-stamping the directions of our own preferences. In fact, Moses's story unfolds over a *century* of careful discernment. There are great periods of silence during which the activities of God are limited. Moses only comes to know God's plans after two-thirds of his life have been spent!

Answering the call does not entitle one to a monopoly of God's power. Some who have answered the call conduct themselves with shamanistic authority as though they have God at their fingertips. Careful listening and discernment of God's meaning in the silence is as important as listening for God's voice. Long periods of silence may trigger our finite minds to believe that our call is over when what it really means is that a season is beginning. Long periods of silence can be interpreted as the end of an era. God uses them to prepare us for something new. Regardless of timing, God's reassuring presence comes to those whom he calls (see 2 Peter 3:8–9).

Closing Thoughts

Over the years as one who answered the call, there have been many times when I felt that I failed in my calling to go where God wanted me to go or to do what he wanted me to do. This false sense of disobedience is quickly restrained by the idea that the calling is not to a place or a type of service. The calling is about *obedience to a person*. The deeper I press in to the calling, the closer I get to the Caller! Our calling is first to be obedient followers of Christ, next to pursue holy living, and *then* to live our vocations.

Rev. Gideon de Jong
Associate Pastor
Saint John's Church of the Nazarene
Berlin, Germany

I do not believe many people were taken by surprise when I told them I was going to Bible college to prepare for pastoral ministry. Some might not have been surprised because they thought it fit me or because I was the fifth of my siblings (including in-laws) to take this step. But all of us have our own individual calling, our own distinct story. My story and testimony are a tribute both to the way my parents raised me and to the influence that friends, Sunday school teachers, camp counselors, youth leaders, pastors, and professors have had on who I have become.

I Am Called

For forty years now my parents have been living in the same house in the seaport city of Rotterdam, The Netherlands, not too far from the stadium that is home to the Feyenoord Rotterdam football (soccer) team. Sometimes we could hear the cheering in our backyard, and my father and I went to various games. In the early years of their marriage my parents, both from Protestant homes, attended a Reformed church, but after a couple of years, they were introduced to the Church of the Nazarene. My siblings and I all grew up in the Rotterdam Church of the Nazarene; we were dedicated there as infants and baptized as believers.

My parents introduced me to the faith by their spiritual example, which is the best gift a parent can give a child. From my birth, they have read Scripture with me, prayed with me, taken me to church, and brought me to children's camps, youth groups, and teen camps. Before booking our holidays, my parents always checked the dates of church camps first, to make sure we wouldn't miss them. During my last children's camp, on Pentecost Sunday, I received Jesus Christ as my Lord and Savior. At the age of fourteen, I was baptized. My parents laid the foundation for my ministry by bringing me up the way they did.

In 1998, my brother, sister-in-law, and one of my brothers-in-law graduated from European Nazarene College, then in Büsingen, Switzerland. My mother recalls I once said to her that I would never follow them to Bible college. However, throughout high school, my belief that God was also calling me to pastoral ministry only grew stronger. My family and our pastor, who had joined me in praying for God's guidance, confirmed that I should go to Bible college.

If Necessary, Use Words

My parents dropped me off at European Nazarene College on their way to a vacation. Yet the first week did not quite go as I anticipated. I became sick for a couple of days and remember lying in bed and wishing my parents would pick me up on their way home. But of course, the illness passed, and I decided to stay. There I was, pretty much in the middle of nowhere with a bunch of students and professors from literally all over the world.

All who have lived in an intercultural setting probably agree that these experiences can often be challenging and tiring, but they can also be incredibly enriching. Throughout the years, I have even come to believe that one can only get to know one's own culture after living in another culture. Due to my numerous intercultural exchanges in college, I have learned about Northern European culture that we are quite rational. We tend to think things through endlessly, often out loud and with others. The danger here is that actual practice runs short.

Three quotes that I stumbled across during my time in college have stuck with me. The first, with which our preaching professor opened his very first class, is attributed to St. Francis of Assisi: "Preach the gospel at all times. If necessary, use words." The second was presented at a EuNC Leadership Conference and is a line from the song "Where Is the Love?" by the Black Eyed Peas: "Can you practice what you preach?" And the third one goes like this: "If you want to become a better person, surround yourself with people who are better than you." These quotes encouraged me to look for a mentor, someone who would inspire me in my pursuit of holiness.

During the first couple years, I developed a mentor relationship with a fellow student who was much older. After he graduated, I asked one of the professors to become my mentor. Both of them were examples to me in their words and deeds, often just in small things.

Testify to the Life and Resurrection of Our Lord Jesus Christ

My wife and I got to know each other at European Nazarene College. After graduating, she wanted to pursue a second degree, which was easier for her to do in her native country. Therefore, it became clear to us early on that we would need to call Germany our home once we married. We settled in Berlin, where she could get her degree and I could serve a Nazarene church. Choosing Berlin was, in many ways, a leap of faith. Right after our wedding we got the news that my wife had been accepted to the university and that I had been accepted as an associate pastor at a Nazarene church in Berlin. In addition, it took time for us to find an apartment and for me to learn a new language and culture. Nonetheless, the church was very welcoming and affirming. Eventually I was transferred to a different Berlin church.

On one hand, being a pastor comes with some automatic disadvantages and challenges. It can be hard to deal with certain expectations while assuming a prophetic responsibility. It can also be hard, at times, to distinguish between cultural traits that are simply different, and those that need to be addressed. On the other hand, I consider it a true privilege to join others on their spiritual journeys. I care about my people, and I always feel humbled when others tell me how God uses me to bring the good news.

At this point, we are not sure yet what fulfilling God's call to ministry will look like after my wife finishes her degree—whether we will stay in Germany or move to another country. Nevertheless, we can only conclude when looking back that God has led us gracefully throughout the years, which assures us that God will continue to do so in the future. Frequently we pray like Jesus in Luke 22:42, "Not my will, but yours be done." May our very lives testify to the life and resurrection of our Lord Jesus Christ.

Rev. Rod DeVore

Family Involvement Specialist
Metro Nashville Public Schools
Nashville, Tennessee

"Whoever wants to become great among you must be your servant, and whoever wants to be first must be slave of all." —Mark 10:43a–44

Our family dinner table was the site of a peculiar gathering. This very common dining room table became a place for extraordinary experiences. As our family spent time together discussing the routine, mundane realities of life, we were introduced to a way of living in the world. At our home, there was always an empty chair for our neighbors to join this sacred time. Those who joined us were from diverse backgrounds. Some of these people were abrasive and rude, while others left a striking example of humility and grace. My parents created space for me to discover and value the beauty of God's strange and peculiar people. At the table, I learned manners that encouraged attentive listening, acceptance, and service. We listened to odd stories, we embraced unconventional requests and sometimes demands, and we made sure our neighbors were satisfied. These practices connected me to the most vulnerable part of humanity. As our very basic needs were met, we found a commonality that allowed us to look into the eyes of strangers and affirm that their stories were sacred and that *every* story mattered.

Throughout the ministry of my parents, the contexts changed, but our table manners remained the same. Each new place introduced me to people of diverse racial, ethnic, and socioeconomic backgrounds. We stepped into the mud and muck of the world as the realities of difference in America pressed on our hearts and minds. These dichotomies pushed our family beyond our sense of comfort and safety into moments of pain and suffering. By God's grace, we journeyed through the residual effects of social construction to affirm the identity of every person as a child of God. These moments of openness and acceptance stirred our hearts and minds to imagine a different way of living in the world. The site of a common meal brought together the memory of what Jesus has done for all creation and the hope of the coming reign of Jesus.

The faithfulness of my parents to guide our family by this alternative narrative left an imprint on my soul that chased after me while I spent a lot of time chasing other voices. The pervasive notions of power, strength, accommodation, and usefulness pulled me in directions away from God. I spent a lot of time escaping to avoid the consistent voice that pursued me. I knew in my soul that I longed for something more. I yearned for more than what I was experiencing, more than what I was consuming, more than what I was able to accomplish. During my freshman year at Trevecca Nazarene University, the presence of God's pursuing love became a voice I could no longer ignore.

In college I spent a lot of time with people in the low-income community that surrounds Trevecca's campus. My love for basketball created an entry point into the community and helped me foster a connection with many of the young men. I spent a lot of afternoons and evenings playing basketball and hanging out with kids. This step into their world broke down barriers that allowed me to form authentic relationships of trust and acceptance. I was slowly allowed to see the realities of poverty and black identity in America through their eyes. Their stories led to compelling and convicting reflections on my interpretation of the gospel and the church's response to poverty in America. As I wrestled with these ideas, God began to open my ears to the cries of the prophets, the melodic yearning of the psalmists, the controversy of the cross, and the renewing power of the resurrection. I began to long for wholeness in a broken world. God slowly nurtured in me a passionate desire to be propelled into the world, proclaiming the reconciling and redeeming power of God's love.

God hurled me into ministry opportunities. I became actively involved with urban youth through local community organizations, juvenile court, Big Brothers Big Sisters, and campus initiatives. Along the way, I met my amazing wife, Emily. We formed our relationship while working with a family of four children from a low-income community. In many ways, Emily and I acted as their surrogate parents while their mother worked through the challenges of life. The joy and pain of sharing life with this family evoked a deep sense of compassion. We spent a lot of time with the adopted grandmother of these children, Eileen. Eileen understood the challenges these children faced. She laughed, wept, and disciplined them as they tried to make sense of their world. Even in a state of frailty and poverty Eileen displayed a deep, unconditional love that profoundly impacted a generation. Her compassionate response opened my eyes to a way of caring for my neighbor. I started to understand what it meant to share in the sufferings of others. I saw how the power of presence moves us beyond the categories of *what we possess* and points others to *who possesses us*. This encounter nourished my soul in ways that allowed me to be open to the path God desired for my life.

My theological education introduced me to present and historical voices that shaped my imagination. The patience of my professors to walk with me as I struggled with new ideas and realities of the gospel changed my life forever. They helped me hear the gospel in ways that demanded a life of service to God's kingdom. I was challenged to share my life with those who stand on the periphery of society, the outcast and disenfranchised. These heavy conversations regarding God's calling were coupled with the experience of serving in a community-based afterschool program. As I walked back and forth between the two worlds, I was able to connect threads of knowledge that refined my notion of ministry.

Working with youth challenged the calling on my life. These young people were so hardened and angry that I went home most days wondering what God was doing. Was God really working through me to impact the lives of these young people? They verbally abused me; they threatened to hit or shoot me. All forms of logic and reason pointed me toward doing something else. However, I begin to realize that my illogical step into their community was as hard for them to embrace as it was for me. The same questions echoed in our minds: *What do they want from me? How long will they be here? Why do they care?*

The clashing perceptions of intent, and our competing classifications, led us to reshape our lives together through the conflict, controversy, and connections we faced. God's love guided us to accept our wounds and voice our pain in ways that revealed our commonality as children of God. We would never have imagined that the power of the Holy Spirit would work through shared meals, porch conversations, and basketball games to embrace an interconnected life that was drawing us into right relationship with God and each other. This ministry of reconciliation taught me how to fully grasp why we are here and who we are called to be for Christ and the church.

Along the path of ordained ministry, I have come to rest in the promise of the new creation, which allows me to live a life of service without the burden of unrealistic expectations, self-loathing, and inadequacy. I have confidence in the promise that God is working in and through me to serve God's kingdom. This posture nurtures hope in the power of God's love to transform communities of faith among us and in the expectation of the reign of God in the coming kingdom. As my life is stretched between the present and coming kingdom, my conception of ministry continues to be shaped as the Holy Spirit works in and through community. I continue to sit at the table with this peculiar gathering of people to laugh, cry, and pray for God's guidance as we seek to serve God's kingdom.

Rev. Shawna Songer Gaines and Rev. Dr. Timothy R. Gaines
Chaplain and Assistant Professor of Religion
Trevecca Nazarene University
Nashville, Tennessee

Shawna's Calling

One Sunday night I sat in the front row of our church, hand raised, ready to ask my pastor dad all the questions racing through my six-year-old mind after Bible study. Afterward, a man from the congregation saw me in the foyer and asked, "What do you want to be when you grow up?"

Without hesitation I responded, "A preacher, just like my dad." I had not had a formal moment of calling or an altar experience at that point. My answer was simply the blunt honesty of a young imagination that had already been captivated by grace.

It was my mother, who answered a call to ministry later in life, who recalls what she heard that man say to me: "Well, maybe you'll make a good preacher's wife someday." It is only by the grace of God that those harmful and dismissive words did not lodge themselves in my memory. What I do remember is my mother pulling me aside and, with no malice toward that brother in Christ, simply affirming that my response to God's call didn't necessarily need to take the shape of that man's expectations.

Being a pastor's wife is no easy task, and I know because my mom was one of the best. I watched her handle the demands and expectations with grace and seeming ease. But I also began to sense that my calling was more to the service of the church itself. Looking at the roles that appeared open to me, I wondered if I would work with children, youth, women, or in evangelism. And as I struggled to see myself in any of those roles, I became increasingly anxious. When I heard these roles recited to me time after time, I didn't sense that grace-filled *yes!* that my six-year-old heart so easily offered up in response to God's call to serve.

Finally, one night at a family camp service, after the preacher finished his sermon, I was compelled to visit the altar. The grace of God had been calling me since childhood, but that night was a significant moment of surrendering to the unknown of God's future. I didn't know which ministry role would be open to me. I didn't know which college I would attend or what major I would declare. There was no life map in my hands. I left all those expectations at the altar that night and walked away full of grace, willing to go where the Spirit would lead.

I didn't see women teaching and preaching until I was in college. And then it was as if the pieces of my calling puzzle were slowly coming together, spurring my imagination to conceive of the possibilities of what ministry could look like for someone like me.

I also, in college, met the man who would share and shape this call with me.

Tim's Calling

When I was sixteen I received a call to ministry in an open field where my church was hoping to one day construct a building. Until it was built, we used a flatbed truck trailer as a platform and held outreach services in the open air under the branches of a sprawling oak tree. A pastor from another local church was preaching that day, though I can't recall the topic of his message. What I do know is that the Spirit was speaking to me. It wasn't an audible voice. I was gripped by the goodness of what God was calling the church to be, and I knew that calling extended to me.

Of course, service to the church wasn't entirely unfamiliar to me. When you grow up in a church like mine, service comes with membership. When I was a sophomore in high school, our family moved from a comfortable, mid-sized church to a smaller congregation in a neighboring town. Our new church family was vibrant and loving, but we didn't have many of the amenities from our previous setting. Our pastor was bivocational. There was no youth pastor. There was no worship band. There was not even a sound system. There *was* decent carpet in the building, though (depending on where you stood).

As a young teenager, I was frustrated by what this church couldn't offer me, but some wise counsel from my parents directed me to consider what I might offer to the church. There wasn't a youth pastor, so I began asking other teenagers in the church if they'd like to put something together. There was no worship band, so I signed up to take piano lessons. The incredible part, though, was that my pastor made a place for me to serve. I may have only known two songs after three months of lessons, but we sang those songs every week until I learned more. It wasn't masterful, but the church seemed more concerned with giving young people a place to grow and serve than with having a polished music program or a flashy youth ministry. The Spirit called me through those opportunities and through the church's humble willingness. And so, when our newly formed worship band brought their instruments out to an old truck trailer in the middle of a dusty field, I was already vaguely familiar with the voice of the Spirit who calls.

I enrolled in college the following year, studying theology and ministry, and continued to look for opportunities to be involved and to serve. In those years I met a young woman who was also exploring a call to ministry.

Called Together

"What does that look like, exactly?" people ask us when they learn that we have served as co-pastors. Most of the time, they are curious about the division of responsibilities and tasks. We've tried to find efficient answers to those questions, but more than the management of responsibilities, the characteristics of sharing a call with a spouse looks like a lot of mutual submission.

The beautiful thing about our unique situation is that sharing a call with another person becomes part of the calling itself. We are called to more faithful service to the church because every day the execution of that call requires each of us to submit to the other in a free act of love. And that's teaching us more and more about what it means to be called by a God whose life is characterized by free acts of love.

God calls us in and through the ministry of one another because the call to ministry is just as much about the kind of person you're being called to be as it is about the tasks you are being called to execute. Before we ever said, "I do," we agreed that when it came to life and ministry, we would always advocate for each other. Tim would place Shawna's call and desires before his own. Shawna would place Tim's call and desires before her own. To be sure, we haven't always gotten this right, but even in our mistakes, we are called to greater depths of faithfulness as we recognize, acknowledge, and take seriously the other person's call to ministry.

Just a few months into our first co-pastor assignment, we had the rare opportunity to go on a date the night before a church event. During our conversation on the way to dinner, we realized that we had each assumed that the other one would be willing stay home from the church event the next day to care for our son. We both assumed incorrectly. The insecurities stemming from each of our inability to acknowledge God's call upon the other were thinly veiled by the words we exchanged that night.

Date night was ruined.

But God's grace was enough to help us recognize that each of us was called, that both callings were real and good, and that we each needed to acknowledge that goodness in submitting our desires to Christ's lordship. Tim is a pastor *and* a pastor's husband. Shawna is a pastor *and* a pastor's wife. By God's grace, we are each becoming better in both of those roles of servant leadership and loving support.

And on that ruined date night, we came to a deeper understanding of the nature of our calling. Slowly, co-pastoring helped us to take the call of Ephesians 5:21 seriously—to submit ourselves to the lordship of Christ and to the calling on both of our lives to work alongside each other in a shared life of humble and reverent submission. God is calling in the calling of another person. Thanks be to God.

Rev. Stephanie Johnson
Co-Pastor
Kennewick Church of the Nazarene
Kennewick, Washington

As a child everyone dreams about what they want to be when they grow up. I knew that I loved people and loved God. Growing up in a Christian home with parents and extended family members who devoted their lives to Christ reminded me we have one life to live. My desire was to serve God. This did not mean it would necessarily be full-time ministry. I knew well the importance of laypeople who give their lives to ministry. I had seen family members be used by God in both capacities, and I wanted to hear clearly what God's calling was for my life.

My mom became a pastor after I finished sixth grade, so I spent a lot of time at the church. I remember sleeping on the floor of her office on early summer mornings, attending prayer meetings at 5:00 a.m. when I could barely keep my eyes open, and teaching in any class that needed it. My desire was to be used by God, and I had a passion for the church from an early age. I had experienced God's goodness, and I felt everyone should have that opportunity.

My call to full-time ministry was confirmed over time. As a pastor's child, I feared that if I went into full-time ministry people would think it was because of my mom. On the other hand, she *was* my mentor, and I was reminded that we are wired very similarly. But still, I wanted to be sure my call to ministry had everything to do with God's call on my life. I saw both the good and bad days of ministry. I saw the phone calls she took late at night. I saw the threat of burnout. I knew that if God was calling me to this life, it would be beautiful and rewarding but also challenging, and it would have to be confirmed by God.

God began working on my heart in adolescence. I remember moments with God when I clearly felt I was being called to ministry. As a junior in high school, my family moved to another state because my mom took a new pastoral position. This move radically changed my spiritual life. My dependence on God and spiritual growth took on a new look on a completely different level. I had opportunities to serve in different ways as my calling and devotion to the church increased. However, as I prepared for college, I continued to wrestle with declaring a major. Though it may have been clear to others, I had to be able to answer the question, *Could I do anything else and be fulfilled?* If the answer was yes, then perhaps it was not a call from God to full-time ministry in the church. In my freshman year, I decided to test my fulfillment potential from another field by majoring in education and minoring in religion at Northwest Nazarene University.

At the end of my first semester of college, I had an accident that almost left me paralyzed. We built a ramp to jump while we were tubing, and I landed badly on my back. I remember my mom telling me later that, in the exact moment the accident happened, God had impressed upon her a need to pray for my back and the organs in my body on a level she had never experienced. I know now this was no coincidence. After experiencing this miracle, I gained a new perspective. I had plenty of time to pray and evaluate my life while stuck in a back brace and on bed rest. No longer did I need to put out fleeces for God. The answer was clear.

There have been moments when I questioned how the logistics would work out. One of those moments happened in the fall of my sophomore year of college. I met a guy who later became my husband. He was a philosophy and religion major with a call to full-time ministry. I remember many late-night talks. How would God ever work this out? Should we end our relationship? How would two people, each with a separate call to full-time ministry, do it? We knew we wouldn't pastor separate churches, but the idea of co-pastors was not common at that time. We decided to proceed in faith and believe that God would provide.

After graduating from college, we both had individual calls and offers to full-time ministry positions. However, we didn't have any calls for us together. My husband felt it was the right time for me to accept a position as the elementary pastor at Crossroads Church of the Nazarene in Chandler, Arizona. After visiting, meeting with church leadership, and praying about where God wanted us, we both felt this was where God was leading. However, this decision meant I would be able to be in full-time ministry but not my husband. We prayed that someday God would allow us both to be paid full-time for the roles we felt called to do.

A few years later, our lead pastor at Crossroads approached my husband about a pastoral position on staff. My husband joined the staff full-time, and we were reminded that God is faithful. God has affirmed his call on both our lives. We continue to thank God as we look back on the years of uncertainty.

In the ten years we spent at Crossroads, I had the privilege of serving in three pastoral positions. I thoroughly enjoyed each position, and God stretched and used me in different ways in each role. I am reminded that the call of God on my life has always been to be in step with whatever God has for that moment. Sometimes I didn't understand what was next or why I was in a specific role, but as the years went on, I was always able to look back and see God's hand in everything.

Toward the end of our time at Crossroads, God began to stir a feeling in my husband and me that a change was coming. The change God was preparing us for was to be co-pastors. It is always difficult to think about leaving when you love serving in your current assignment. We prayed and decided that, if co-pastoring was the call God had for us, a district superintendent would reach out to us. We did not go out and search for new or different positions because we were content with our current positions. Two days later, we received a call from a district superintendent asking if we were interested in being co-pastors in Kennewick, Washington. So we embarked on another new journey.

I have no doubt that God calls. God burned a desire in my heart as a young child to serve in full-time ministry. There is nothing else I could do to be fulfilled other than follow after God's heart and desire for my life. There are days I have to look back and be reminded of this call because ministry can be exhausting, trying, and difficult, but God is faithful.

My call to ministry will continue to be shaped and changed. My call to serve God with every ounce of my being will continue in whatever capacity God has for me. God has confirmed my call through continued faithfulness, giftings, and the encouragement of others. I have no idea what the future holds, but I am thankful God equips those who are called. I will live in obedience and pray God uses me in whatever way God sees necessary for the seasons of my life.

Rev. Ignacio and Rev. Litzy Pesado
District Superintendent and Pastors
Spain District and Barcelona Church of the Nazarene
Barcelona, Spain

Ignacio

I grew up in a missionary home. Indirectly, I was always involved in ministry. I was born and lived in Argentina for only two years. After that, we lived in different countries serving the Lord. As a result, I learned firsthand about ministry and the church. Service and ministry have always been part of my life. However, I never saw myself dedicating my life to full-time ministry, but my parents saw it. When I was a teenager, we moved to Spain to serve as missionaries. My plan was to become a veterinarian or a history professor. It never occurred to me to be a pastor.

When I was eighteen years old, my family and I were invited to a youth conference in Cordoba, Argentina. I was particularly excited to visit my family and friends there, since we did not get to see them often. The trip was going to last two weeks. The first week was great because the conference hadn't started yet, and we were just having fun. But the second week arrived, and I was not very excited about the conference. For me, the conference was just the boring part of the vacation. I met up with old friends and made new friends too, so I started to have some fun, but I was not expecting anything in particular. I had been to many conferences, camps, services, and church-related events, and this conference was just one more.

On the last day of the conference, the preacher talked convincingly about God's call. I remember sitting there waiting for the altar call so I could pray. I felt God calling me to consecrate my life to him and to serve him without conditions. I felt like my heart was burning in desire to serve God and to let him do whatever he wished in my life. After the prayer, I felt relieved, and from that point on I had a clear call from God to serve full-time.

Litzy

I was born and raised in Bolivia. My childhood included being involved in the church. My family and I attended church regularly. I was the typical child who never missed VBS, Sunday school, or camps, and I attended a Christian school. Since my childhood I remember my mum always praying for me and my future ministry. She always told me she had dedicated me to serve God and to preach his word—at which I just nodded every time, to be polite. I never thought her prayers would come to be true.

One summer I was preparing and packing for youth camp. The camp was very special for me because I was getting baptized. Most of my family was attending. I was excited. The first night the preacher talked about his call to ministry and how it had changed his life forever. The second night, he talked about God calling us to be prepared to give him an answer. I felt something in my heart, but I was hesitant to believe that God was actually calling me. The last night he preached about Moses giving excuses to God's call, and I realized he was talking about me! I went to the altar and asked God to make clear that what I was feeling was actually from him. I was in my last year of school, and I had plans for my life, so if God was going to call me, he needed to explain to me what that meant! That was my excuse.

Later that year, at our church anniversary, God gave me the confirmation I needed. There was a huge world map covering the altar wall. The preacher talked about missions. The whole celebration was about missions. At that time I knew I had to give an answer to God. I knew God really was interested in me and calling me to serve him full-time. The pastor prayed and said that God was sending people into the world. My heart burned. I wanted to go. Finally I was sure God was sending me out into the world to preach in his name. All my doubts immediately disappeared. All my plans became nothing. All I wanted was to do God's will.

Ministering Together

We met in Madrid, Spain, in 2002. After dating for a year and a half, we both were sure God was sending us to prepare for ministry. We both went to European Nazarene College and studied for four years. During that time, we knew God was calling us to serve and live in Spain. While in school, we saw how God confirmed his will and purpose for our lives. A year later we got married in Spain.

In our last year of school, we had a meeting with the Spain district superintendent, and he asked us to pray about pastoring a church in Barcelona that did not have a pastor, and where we had completed an internship the previous summer. We prayed, and we felt God's leading, so we gladly accepted the challenge.

In 2008 we were assigned as pastors of the Barcelona Church of the Nazarene. Our ministry consists of preaching, teaching, counseling, and ministry to our community. In 2012 Ignacio was also assigned as the new district superintendent of Spain. We journey with the other pastors on our district, encouraging and supporting their ministry and service. We also serve with an education program for our district to help people answer to their call to ministry. We are seeing how God is still calling people to ministry today.

We thank God every day for the wonderful opportunities he has given us to serve him. It has not always been easy. There have been several times we felt we were not going to be able to finish the race. And we know there are more obstacles ahead. But we know that the God who called us is faithful. When God called us, we did not know all the details, but we can look back and see his faithfulness over the years. God has not shown us his entire plan. God led us, step by step, through faith.

Rev. Andrew and Rev. Simone Twibell
Assistant District Superintendent
Church of the Nazarene Chicago Central District
Bourbonnais, Illinois

Simone

It was just another ordinary chapel day at Olivet Nazarene University, but for me, chapel was more than just an institutional requirement. During this particular phase of my life, it was a personal necessity. Our chaplain, Dr. Michael Benson, had begun a series titled "Do You Know the Plan?" Over the course of that semester, Chaplain Benson repeatedly asked this question, convinced that eighteen-year-old freshmen had the intellectual capacity and spiritual acumen to offer an answer with unshakable certainty.

On this particular Wednesday, Dr. Benson preached an inspiring message from Joshua 4. It would have been easier at the time if the message regarding my life plans had come through on a practical level, providing a set of logical next steps for me. But the simple question relentlessly came: *Do you know the plan?* How could I possibly know the plan God had for my life at such an early age? I certainly had dreams, passions, and ideas about how God might use me, but I had never received an audible call like Isaiah or a theophany experience like Moses.

Growing up on the mission field, I always knew I would serve the Lord. When I was seven, I remember telling my parents I would become a missionary to Africa so I could feed hungry children. Throughout my developmental years, I believed my future would involve serving God in some capacity on the foreign field. But then, when I came to the United States as a student, I never even considered the possibility of becoming a missionary to this great country. Yet, as the chaplain preached and as my mind was bombarded with all sorts of possible responses, one single word rose above the ca-

88

cophony and brought absolute clarity: *Christ*. At that moment the congruence of meaning completely stilled the chaos in my heart and mind. As the message drew to a close, we in the congregation were invited to pick up a rock from the altar and write on it the plan we believed God had for us. Satisfied with the sense of direction and revelation I had received, I confidently wrote "Christ" on that little rock, knowing that, from that day forward, he would indeed be my plan. My plan was not a career or a profession but a person.

During my senior year, I was elected chaplain of the senior class and given a local minister's license at Wildwood Church of the Nazarene in Kankakee, Illinois. Inspired by the godly lifestyle of my resident director and the revival services at Olivet, I sought to respond to the plan God had revealed to me three years earlier. I began to read many of the spiritual classics, spent more time in the Word, and practiced constant prayer. I experienced a time of powerful personal revival, and out of this renewal came the desire to preach. As God continued to move in my life, I could sense his heart for a hurting world that needed the hope of Christ.

After graduating from college, I knew I needed to continue my theological education to prepare myself for the task of sharing Christ. While pursuing my master's degree at Olivet, I began to date Andrew. Two years later we were married and began to share the hope of Christ with a hurting world.

Andrew

Why am I here? What's my calling? What's my true purpose in life? Throughout various stages of life, these questions had been my constant companions. Interestingly, it was the most ordinary moments that often gave rise to my greatest existential uncertainties—dinnertime conversations with family, a reflective moment with a friend, or an early-evening walk through the woods. More often than not, like a tantalizingly elusive butterfly, such thoughts refused to linger, touching down just long enough to be felt but never long enough to be captured. *Truly, why am I here?*

As the years have progressed, I find myself enjoying more frequently the quiet moments when the confluence of clarity and time provide an opportunity for purposeful contemplation. I am reminded during such moments of the way in which the Lord has faithfully taken my hand, guided my steps, and confirmed his call on my life.

I am blessed to have been raised in a Christian home with happily married parents and three older brothers. I distinctly remember accepting Jesus's call into an intentional personal relationship with him when I was eight. I consider it a true gift of God that I remember so clearly that moment when my mother and father knelt with me in prayer at my bedside. I am eternally grateful for salvation at such an early age.

Yet not too many years passed before I began facing the dreaded question of what I would "be" when I grew up. As college loomed in the near future I decided to begin telling my well-meaning but overly curious friends that I had decided to become a doctor. Receiving a great amount of affirmation in response, I soon enrolled as a biology and premedical student at Olivet Nazarene University.

Externally, my medical pursuits were successful, but internally a storm had begun to brew. Unconsciously at first, but with a progressively greater sense of urgency, I perceived a distinct leading toward the pursuit of theological studies. Yet, having already completed a significant portion of my biology degree, I actively suppressed this impression and continued undeterred toward my medical career.

In the final year of my undergraduate studies, however, everything changed. A significant romantic relationship abruptly dissolved. My oldest brother, who was also my closest friend, passed away. Secrecy and deceit eroded the very foundations of my most treasured relationships. Any one of these events could understandably cause a significant reevaluation of one's life direction, but together they were almost too much to bear. In a matter of months, every pillar on which I had established my carefully constructed existence had collapsed.

Reflecting upon this time in my life years later, a wise counselor once told me, "Sometimes the Lord loves us enough to provide multiple crises for us." And truly, it was through the rebuilding period following these personal upheavals that the Lord relentlessly impressed upon my heart the need for personal reformation and theological preparation.

As I prayerfully considered my future, the Spirit began to bring to light some of the darkest places of my heart, places I had kept tucked away from the world and from myself. The Spirit revealed how distorted and deluded my thinking had become, how I had conflated career goals and personal achievements with my primary calling. The Spirit exposed the way in which I had slipped into a deadly form of functionalism, identifying my life's value by my grades, work, and future success. Most painfully I discovered that I had exchanged the primary principles of devotional living in Christ and relational strengthening in community for isolation and insulation from the guidance of the Holy Spirit.

As the reality of my true self came fully into view, I knelt beside my bed once more, this time to wholeheartedly consecrate every aspect of my life to the Father. As I exchanged my brokenness—career plans, family, relationships—for God's wholeness, I wept mightily at the realization that the Lord was beginning a new work in me. And as I consecrated my life to him, the Father sanctified me wholly for the fulfillment of his purposes and blessed me with an inner peace that comes from full submission to his Spirit.

In subsequent years, I have recognized a dramatic shift in my life values, perception of calling, understanding of mission, and focus on holiness. As opposed to an isolated state of selfishness, I have found true joy in following after Christ, surrounding myself with a community that speaks truth into my life. Rather than perceiving my career as my calling, I have come to admit that, first and foremost, we are called not to do something or be somewhere but, rather, to serve Jesus.

Throughout the past several years, Simone and I have had the blessing of serving in various ministerial roles that have confirmed our calling. While serving as a resident director at Olivet Nazarene University, the Lord revealed to me my gifts in the areas of leadership and counseling. During these years, Simone served as the pastor of a Hispanic ministry at Kankakee First Church of the Nazarene, where she discovered her gifting in the areas of preaching and teaching. Soon after, we followed the Spirit's leading to Kentucky to pursue further studies at Asbury Theological Seminary. While attending Asbury we were pleasantly surprised by the opportunity to continue our ministerial service as co-pastors of the Nicholasville Grace Community Church of the Nazarene.

More than ever before, we recognized our limitations and utter incapability to fulfill the Lord's work without the infilling of the Holy Spirit and the humility required to partner together in God's ministry as husband and wife. Recognizing our own proclivities toward independence, we have learned to allow the Lord to break us of all pessimism by inviting his presence and purpose to be the guiding force behind all he has called us to do. With each passing day, as God continues to engineer circumstances that confirm his calling on our lives as witnesses to his kingdom, we are reminded that our call is first and foremost to himself. After all, that is truly why we are here.

Rev. Mike Yost
Pastor
Longview Church of the Nazarene
Longview, Washington

My childhood was unremarkable. I was born to parents who are devoted followers of Christ. I grew up in church. I was part of one of those families who were at the church building just about any time it was open. However, I grew up with only a vague sense of what it meant to be a follower of Jesus Christ. For a long time I considered following Jesus to consist of faithfully attending church services. Following Christ was somewhat like going to school or visiting the dentist every six months. It was merely something I was supposed to do because it was good for me. I enjoyed going to church. I had lots of friends there, but I had no passion for Christ, no heart for his kingdom.

It was not until early in high school that I considered there might be something more to following Christ than just attending. I began to realize, through the influence of mentors in my life, that following Christ was about relationship, not attendance. So I dove headlong into that relationship. I invested in any way I could in following Jesus. Oddly, this investment mostly consisted of doing *more* for the sake of Jesus, which actually meant that I spent more time at church, so I still perceived the physical reality of being *at* church as a relationship with Jesus. I did spend a little more time in prayer and Bible study, but there was still something missing in my relationship with Jesus, and I felt great despair.

As the possibility of college drew near, I began to ask myself questions about my future. I wondered what I was to do with the rest of my life. The only thing I really enjoyed doing was going to church. At the same time, I felt a great void in my soul, as if I were missing something in my life. I recall thinking that God was asking something of me, but I had no idea what it was. In retrospect, I believe this was what God's call sounded like, but at the time I had no idea what was going on. I spent every opportunity I could in prayer, often weeping at the altar in confusion and frustration. I did not know what more I could do to make God happy!

In one such moment of prayer, a trusted mentor approached me and inquired as to what had driven me to the altar. I told him the story of what had been going on in my life, and as he listened a smile crept across his face. It was the kind of smile someone gives you when they know something you don't know. In this case, the smile also meant he had struggled with the same things, had faced the same challenges, and knew what I was going through. Though the memory of his response is a great comfort to me now, it only made me mad at the time.

He probably sensed my frustration because he quickly said, "I think I know what's going on. I believe I know what God may be calling you to. However, this is not something I can tell you. It is something you must hear for yourself. Continue to seek God and to pray, and when you think you know, come and find me."

Thanks for nothing, I thought. I wanted answers, but no answers were given.

The story of my calling reminds me of the story of Samuel's calling as told in 1 Samuel 3. Samuel is just as confused as I was at first, and God calls several times before Samuel truly hears and understands. When I was seventeen, I heard the Lord speak and call me to ministry, but I did not know what that meant. I had not learned *how* to hear the voice of God. My wise mentor knew what I was hearing, but he also knew I had to listen and hear for myself what God was saying. As the months went on, I did not have a great epiphany, but the idea dawned on me like a slow sunrise. I do not know exactly when I realized it, but at some point I did. I understood and believed that the Lord was calling me into pastoral ministry as a vocation—a thought that terrified me.

I enrolled at Northwest Nazarene University and, later, Nazarene Theological Seminary to prepare to be a pastor. Up until my first year in seminary I was responding to God because God had called. The one who claimed me had called, and I was obeying, even if I had no idea how I would become a pastor and preacher. During my first year in seminary I had the opportunity to study Paul's first letter to Corinth. Before that time, I loved Jesus and wanted to follow him anywhere, but in seminary, I fell in love with the church. In studying 1 Corinthians, I began to see a vision of the in-breaking kingdom of God. God does not want us merely to attend church; God wants passionate disciples who are led by the Spirit of God, ruled by love, and committed to the transforming message of the crucified Messiah.

At various points in my life, I have had trusted mentors and teachers to lead and guide me and share a greater vision of God and of what God is doing and of what God has called God's people to become. I have had many Elis in my life, many people who have encouraged me to listen closely to the voice of the Lord calling. Therefore, I see my role as a minister to be one who serves in this way to others. I do not see my call as one who gives answers; rather, I direct others to quiet down and learn to say, "Speak, Lord, for your servants are listening." As we allow space for God to speak, God will give us a vision of how we might join in God's work in the in-breaking kingdom. One of my greatest joys as a pastor is walking with others as they begin to hear the call of God on their lives—many for the first time. God continues to give me a vision for the in-breaking kingdom so the church might be an agent of transformation in God's created world.

At Longview Nazarene, we are committed to a two-fold purpose—to love God and to love people. This simple mission lies at the very root of God's kingdom. What initially drew me to Longview

Church was its strategic physical location, allowing opportunities to connect with nearly every demographic of our community. Our church is able to connect people with the crucified and resurrected Messiah in order to offer a place of healing, a place of transformation, and a place of community. We are a place where people can come to meet Jesus and experience the in-breaking kingdom of God.

Experienced
Leader
Narratives

Experienced leaders are women and men who are in the sweet spot of their ministry calling. They have a proven track record of service by demonstrating their knowledge and skills for effective ministry. They have followed their call to ministry for many years and have become mature, wise, and respected ministers of the gospel. They are significant influencers in their ministries as they equip, develop, and unleash the next generation of God-called ministers. As you read the stories of these experienced leaders, we hope you will see how they are being faithful to their calling and how they embody the call in their lives and ministries.

Rev. John Haines
Eurasia Regional Education Coordinator
Church of the Nazarene
Schaffhausen, Switzerland

When I was eight years old, I was in a Sunday school class taught by a woman who had surpassed eighty years of age and suffered from severe arthritis. She walked with the help of two canes and shuffled her feet. It was a distinctive sound that still plays in my memory. I was like any other eight-year-old boy: I would rather have been anywhere but there. Sitting in that Sunday school class, I always drifted to other places and possibilities. But at the end of each class, my teacher shuffled over to the door, opened it just a bit, and leaned against the door post with one hand, propping herself up on her canes with the other. She formed something of a bridge spanning that narrow escape passage. From there, she said the closing prayer and, when finished, lifted her head and winked at us. That was our cue to escape, and several of us jumped to run out. Just as we reached the door, she dropped around us, wrapped us in a big hug, and said, "Remember, Miss Dietrich will be praying for you this week!"

On the morning that I accepted the salvation of Jesus, I don't remember much from the service, but I do remember my eight-year-old heart feeling like it would break. I felt drawn to the altar to pray and ask Jesus into my life as Lord and Savior. The only thing I remember other than that simple prayer, over the sound of my own weeping, is the clicking of two canes and the shuffling of feet. I felt my teacher's gnarled hand on my head, and I heard her call out my name in her prayer. Because of her witness, I am part of the kingdom today.

When I was nine years old I felt a deep sense of calling into ministry. I did not understand what that meant or what it might mean for my future. At nine, one usually hardly thinks of the future, but it was all I could think about. My grandparents were both Quaker ministers, and my grandmother often said to me, "Johnny, remember, you are the answer to the prayers of generations before you." From what I could tell, my future connected with the past and the lives of those I did not know. Over and over again, my grandmother's words have rung true in my life and experience. How exciting to think that we are answers to prayers offered generations before.

There was a little hand-painted plaque that hung in my grandparents' home throughout their ministry that displayed an old Quaker saying: *As thou goest, step by step, the way shall open up before thee.* My grandparents often pointed to that plaque and instructed me to walk faithfully, one step at a time, into the future of God's imaginings for me. It was good advice. I owe so much to my grandparents, and I am in the ministry today in large measure because of their holy influence.

When I said yes to God in response to his call upon my life, my pastor at the time came alongside and told me, "If God is calling you, it is not just about your *future*; it is about you being in ministry *today*." What? How could a nine-year-old minister? Could I discover a vocation? With creative imagination and a tender spirit, my pastor encouraged me to preach. He wanted me to go with him to the hospital to pray with the sick and dying. He believed there was great value and influence in the simple prayers of a young heart, and it encouraged the sick, the old, and the dying to know that a child was praying for them. He took me along to serve Communion to the shut-ins who could not come to church.

I was nine years old and serving in ministry. I loved it! Sure, I made my share of mistakes—what child wouldn't? Yet I never recall a single angry or agitated word from my pastor. He encouraged me to keep taking those steps, one by one, into God's call. Again, I am in the ministry today because of the strong mentoring of this pastor and others who invested their lives in mine.

When I finished my studies I was restless because of a growing sense of a whispered, echoed urgency calling me to cross the globe and give my life to others. Calling me to serve people I did not know. I applied to serve as a missionary, but I was rejected because I was a single man. As a response to what I understood to be the unfolding nature of God's call upon my life, I went anyway, even though I was not officially sent. I went from the United States to the United Kingdom to serve in ministries that were as yet unclearly defined. I intended to stay for two years. I've been in Europe now for thirty-six years.

Every ministry role I have accepted and every move I have made seemed like stepping stones along a pathway I could not quite perceive. Yet, what I do now, I could not have done if it weren't for each ministry position along the way that prepared me. We walk this way together. God, who calls us, is with us all along the way. The Spirit, who enables us, is our companion on the road. But don't forget that our way is marked and brightened by the many godly people who faithfully choose to join us with their encouragement, prayers, and gestures of love and support. Where would we be without these good people? The truth is we are inextricably linked to those God brings into our lives to share the road. We are called to help one another form and develop into effective, Christlike ministers in the world.

Maybe we miss opportunities to understand God's call and the best way to fulfill it because we are too busy thinking only about ourselves in the process. It is not about us. And ministry doesn't begin because we arrive on the scene. We are ever joining God in his eternal purposes if we are willing, and we build on the work of generations who have gone before, while at the same time building for the generations yet to come.

In the Wye River Valley, near the borders of England and Wales, stands the ruin of ancient Tintern Abbey. I used to love to visit the site and spend time with the curator of the museum and information center. Once he shared with me about how the abbey was built. Each generation of builders—humble monks who were building a holy, living temple to the Lord—labored faithfully, side by side, until each layer of stone was complete, standing securely on a strong foundation. It took generations to finish the project. The curator said, "Each generation built carefully upon the work of those who were there before them." They practiced their craft with excellence in honor of the Lord and of one another, and taught those who would follow them—a new generation—to continue this labor of love and devotion. All of this, done with the knowledge that they would not see the completion of the work they gave their lives to. What a picture! Our call as Christians is not only unfolding; it is unfinished. We are to be faithful, in our generation, to do all that we can so others may build upon our labors of love and devotion.

The ministry I am engaged in now is not what I expected at the age of nine. It is so much more! I left my home and family, but I have been blessed by an ever-growing diverse and beautiful family in a great big world. I would not exchange what I have been given to regain what I had to give. I have been allowed to teach others along the way that continues to open up before me. I've wrestled with the challenges of changing paradigms, and of learning and living a vital faith. Ministry is a privilege. Have I done all I could or should? I've tried, as best I could discern. However, what matters in my journey is that I continue to dare to walk a way that opens up, and join others as together we journey into God.

This I know: The God who calls is faithful—always!

Rev. Frank Lantei Mills
Pastor and District Superintendent
Church of the Nazarene Ghana North District
Ghana, Africa

I grew up in a Christian home where the Christian life was never practiced. I attended church without any special relationship with Jesus. Christ found me at the age of fifteen, drowning in sin. I accepted Jesus and found rest. I took my decision seriously to follow Christ for the rest of my life and never turn back. At my youthful age, I wanted to tell everyone about Christ and the joy of serving and trusting him. But I wasn't interested in the pastoral profession because I saw how pastors worked selflessly without making much money. I did not want to live that kind of life. I loved to tell people about Jesus, but I did not want to preach. I experienced God's cleansing of sin at the age of twenty. I then had confidence of living a holy life, and I have never regretted this experience. Our God—the God of Abraham—is still alive and with us even today.

I have always had the passion to grow in my relationship with the Lord and to care for my soul. I did this through regular prayer, reading of Scripture, meditating on the Word, fasting, reading good theology books, attending regular church services, leading family devotions, serving in various ministries, loving all people, and spending quality time with God in silence. I was more concerned about my relationship with Jesus than I was about how others related to Jesus. I thought I was more holy, and I withdrew from spending time with friends and others.

After graduating from teacher training college in 1997, I was assigned to teach in a new public school. I frequently found myself teaching the gospel at any available free period. I found joy in teaching the gospel instead of the required academic subjects. This shift was strange to me and to my parents because I had previously spent so much time in isolation with God. Suddenly there was a huge shift from enjoying spending time with God alone to wanting to teach others about God. I began to suspect the Holy Spirit at work in my life. Each time I decided to go out with friends, I asked myself why I was going to waste time with friends when I could be spending that same quality time teaching others about Jesus.

I eventually formed a regular Bible study group that met on Sundays for reading Scripture, sharing testimonies, and participating in worship. Many thought we were a church, even though I saw our group as merely a Bible study group. Many called me "Pastor," but I always corrected them by saying, "I am a group leader, not a pastor." I kept refusing the title *pastor* and preferred to be called the leader. I saw myself as too simple, too young, too poorly educated, and unworthy of being called a pastor.

I thank God for a missionary who helped me identify God's calling upon my life to preach the good news. In several conversations he kept saying, "Frank, God has called you to be a shepherd of his flock; you need to obey and accept this special invitation from the Lord."

I finally accepted the call and got busy in ministry. I found great joy in being busy for the Lord as I planted two churches and served in many district responsibilities. I am regularly filled with hope and joy when I remember that I am part of what God is doing on earth with and for his creation—doing what Scripture says, living a holy life on earth. This is why I will use any available opportunity to help someone know Jesus and be saved and disciple into maturity. Oh! I love to do God's work. I love his ministry. No condition or suffering of any kind can stop me from serving in the kingdom of God.

God saved me and called me to his ministry for a purpose. God wants to use me for his glory through the preaching and teaching ministries of the church. It is a great privilege to be allowed to preach and teach the gospel and see other leaders develop. I do not look upon my calling as difficult or boring work; rather, it is a joy and opportunity to serve the Lord. I am very thankful for God's call upon my life.

I was ordained in 2008 and appointed the first district superintendent of the Ghana North district. My family and I had to leave our home in south Ghana for our new assignment. This new work moved from a pioneering mission field to a regular district. Since 2012, I have served as the youth ministries coordinator for the Africa West field. Recently I was appointed as coordinator/advocate for the youth justice movement in the Africa region. I am also teaching pastors and lay leaders through the Nazarene Theological Institute in the Africa West field.

God called me when I was nobody. God prepared me as I continued to obey his lead. God equipped me and sent me to go make disciples. God walks and works with me in silence, and I am so excited about how God is using me and others to build his kingdom.

Rev. Jennifer Roemhildt Tunehag
Independent Missions Consultant for Human Trafficking
Hässelby, Sweden

Jesus was called a friend of sinners, and this slur is one of the most beautiful names given to Christ. If Jesus is a friend to sinners, then he is not ashamed to be my friend, or to lead me into friendship with others who need healing, deliverance, and the presence of God. My joy and calling have been to take the good news of the gospel to those on the margins of society and the fringes of the church. These are the despised, the outcast, and the public sinners. Growing up, I was intrigued and disturbed when the church appeared to say to a person or group, "The love of God is not for you." It became like a road map for me to follow, and an assertion to refute through the demonstration of that love.

As a child, I remember not wanting to be a princess, a ballerina, or a teacher. I wanted to be a missionary. My mother had come to Alaska as a missionary nurse, and our home was full of stories about children in other lands who had never heard about Jesus and stories of people who didn't have access to the Bible in their own language. I decided there was no job in the whole world cooler than being a "spy for Jesus."

Many twists, turns, and years later, I found myself on the streets of Athens, Greece, where I started a ministry among women and men who are sexually exploited in prostitution and trafficking. It was late when I left the center one night. Our refugee-feeding program had run long, and I was eager to get home—partly because of the hour, partly because of the neighborhood. The area around Omonoia in Athens, Greece, is a nightmare of human misery. Drug addicts purchase and consume their doses, and homeless refugees spill over the sidewalks to fill the streets. Women stand on corners and in shadowy doorways offering their bodies to anyone who can pay.

It is not the kind of place where you want to loiter. But, as I walked toward my trolley that night, a woman caught my attention. She stood in front of a rundown hotel, soliciting customers. Certainly not the first woman I had seen in prostitution in our area, and surely not the only woman working that night. But as I looked at her, something happened. I think it might be something like what Christ felt when it is recorded in Scripture that he saw the crowds and was moved to compassion. I felt like seeing this woman was an invitation, but I was not sure to what. I began to pray. Over several weeks, I asked God to open the door. Even though I was already a missionary, I had no idea how to approach a woman in prostitution! I prayed, "Give me a way to speak to her, Lord." God was not slow in answering.

Another late night, another brisk walk through the neighborhood, and this time several people stood outside the hotel. The group consisted of a few women and one very big man wearing a red skirt. I'm sure he would have been tall even without the heels, but he wore high heels, and a long, blonde wig. As I approached the group, he stepped out into my path. He asked, "You got the time?" I thought, *I hope he means my watch.*

I held out my arm as I walked past so he could read the time on his own. I hadn't gone more than a few steps when God moved again. *This is a very sad man,* God seemed to be saying, and I immediately began to pray as I pushed through the streets toward home, and I could not stop praying. Prayer poured out of me over this man and his life. I felt as if the Spirit of God had been waiting for someone to intercede for him. My urgent feeling was, *I have to go back.* Then came another thought: *That is the stupidest thing I have ever heard! It's eleven o'clock at night in one of the most dangerous neighborhoods in the city. What do you even think is going to happen?*

I paced the sidewalk and argued with God. "If you want me to go back, at least tell me what you want me to do!"

Ask them their names, God said.

I think you will recognize that this is not a complete plan. Still, I was encouraged. This was something I could do! There was only one woman standing in front of the hotel when I returned, but she was the same woman I had seen weeks earlier. "I was on my way home," I told her, "but I felt like God wanted me to come back and talk to you." We talked for a while, and when I left I offered what I had: "I'll be praying for you, Elise."

She grabbed both my hands and said, "Will you pray for me now?"

Startled but willing, I began to pray. As I spoke to the Father, Elise kept whispering: "Yes, Lord. Yes, Lord!"

I didn't know where God was leading, and maybe that was a good thing because I am not sure I would have been ready to embark on a life dedicated to serving women and men in prostitution and victims of human trafficking. But I knew that God loved me, and I wanted to go wherever God led.

That conversation with Elise became the first of hundreds of conversations in Athens and around the world. It looks profoundly hopeful when the church follows Christ into the brokenness of slavery and abuse. It may look like street outreach in Athens, where teams of dedicated women and men continue to build bridges of hope and help to women like Elise. Or it may resemble the courage of evangelical Christians in Spain who approached the major political parties in their country to ask what they were planning to do about prostitution. "If you will draft a legislation that is good for women in Spain," the Christians were told, "we will bring it to Parliament." It may mean creating businesses that embrace God's purposes through prevention, protect the vulnerable, and restore victims of human trafficking.

The situation is hopeful because we are invited, compelled (see 2 Corinthians 5:14) to follow Jesus, who came to seek and to save the lost. As we walk with him in these dark places, we can be confident that the darkness has not, and will not, overcome him.

In my life, Jesus invited me to participate in his purpose and his community. Northwest Nazarene University was one of the first communities where my calling was fanned into flame by professors and leaders like Dr. Irving Laird, Dr. Ralph Neil, and Dr. Gordon Wetmore. My time as an undergrad at NNU and as a graduate student at the Bresee Institute in Los Angeles equipped me with vision and skills to fulfill my calling through wonderful friends and mentors.

Today I serve among diverse groups of people called to Christ's purposes of freedom—businesspeople, lawyers, politicians, church and mission leaders, and ordinary people working out their love for Christ and for others through their lives.

I have helped to forge a community of ministries in Europe consisting of more than two hundred groups and individuals who work together with the European Freedom Network to build a bridge to freedom across forty countries. I am working with others to create job opportunities for vulnerable people through the Freedom Business Alliance, an emerging trade association for those working to fight exploitation through enterprise. I love the work that has been entrusted to me, and I love the One who has given it to me and who walks next to me every day.

It is not clear to me whether I was specifically *called* as a child. When I look back, though, what *is* clear is that something resonated when I encountered the good works that God prepared in advance for me to do (see Ephesians 2:10). May you also know God's good call to those good works!

Rev. Scott Shaw
District Superintendent
Church of the Nazarene Intermountain District
Nampa, Idaho

When I was a boy my mother loved to tell the story about a moment that took place at my birth. It seems that I came into the world screaming with great gusto, which prompted the doctor to declare, "Well, Mrs. Shaw, it looks like you've got yourself another preacher." While her memory always prompted a chuckle from those listening, there was something weighted in that expectation, for if my clan had a family business, it would be identified as pastoral ministry. My grandfathers served as pastors, my father was a pastor, all of the uncles I knew had been or were pastors, and my older brother eventually became a pastor.

It appeared that pastoral ministry was somehow ingrained in our family DNA and that I was destined to fill that role too. With an independent spirit of my own, though, I figured it was time to break the mold. When people asked what I wanted to do when I grew up I began to declare, "Anything but be a pastor!"

Now, don't get me wrong. I had a great experience growing up as a pastor's kid. Through my first eighteen years of life, I developed a deep love for God and came to embrace the church as my extended family. My father spent thirty-two years pastoring the same congregation. Our life in the parsonage was characterized by a good deal of peace and stability. I thoroughly enjoyed life in and around the church, but when it came to my own future, I simply wanted to pursue other things. I had experienced some athletic success and thought it would be enjoyable to have a job where I could go to work in sweats and tennis shoes. I pictured myself serving God as some kind of teacher and coach. I figured this would be a great way to fuel my competitive fire as I mentored young men.

When the time came, I left California and all close family connections and made the trek to the Northwest to pursue my dream. Like trailblazers of the past, I was excited and eager to map a new course and explore new territory. During my first year at Northwest Nazarene College (now University), things came together swimmingly as I went about making new friends and establishing my own identity. I adjusted well to the college experience, pursuing a degree in education, playing both basketball and baseball, and generally having the time of my life.

When I came back as a sophomore, my expectation was to build on my first year's success. But while things continued to go well, there was a unique stirring in my heart. In numerous ways, God probed me with the question, *Are you totally sold out to me?* I began to carry this odd sense that, even though I enjoyed my education classes, something about them didn't seem to fit. Even though the great plan I had made was coming together, I found myself struggling, feeling unfulfilled and dissatisfied. I remember having many discussions with God as I walked around campus, reminding him that while I did love him, I didn't feel that pastoring a church was for me. In his kind and gentle way, God simply kept asking me if I was willing to trust him with all of my life.

My moment of decision came during a midweek chapel service. Dr. William Greathouse spoke on the nature of the fully surrendered life. As I sat listening, Dr. Greathouse's voice became lost in the greater call of God inviting me to place all that I was into his hands. I wrestled with him for quite a few minutes during that service, as I had done so many nights before. I identified all the ways I had already yielded my life to him, but there was this unresolved issue of pastoral service. Would I be willing to embrace that call?

Then, the moment I stepped from my seat to go forward to pray, I knew what was before me. The beautiful thing was that I traded a sense of dread for a sense of freedom. This was not a decision I was making on the basis of my family heritage or my parents' desire. No, I had clearly and personally heard the call of God over my life, and I offered myself in service to him and him alone. In that moment, responding in obedience to his voice was all that mattered.

As I write these words today, I realize I've now been involved in pastoral ministry for more than thirty years, and the central issue of my life really hasn't changed. As a youth pastor, seminary student, and then lead pastor of two churches, my life has always been drawn to the call to obedience. Day by day God has invited me to trust him with a heart and life that are willing to say yes to his leadings. I've discovered that in my life faithfulness must always be a present-tense expression for what I've done in the past and hope to do in the future. God's call over my life has brought with it the promise of his wisdom and strength because I must be willing to offer all of my life to him. That's a critical ministerial lesson, for while I may have little control over where and how many I will serve, I can give my full attention to being faithful, and that has become my central desire.

I sense that my original apprehension and fear relating to God's call upon my life were based on the idea that if I fully followed God's direction, I would somehow sacrifice many of my personal hopes and dreams. In my mind, choosing to serve in pastoral ministry placed limitations on all I wanted to do and be, and invited me to wear a tag or label that would stifle both my personality and potential. What I've discovered is that God knows far better than I do that the gifts, abilities, and interests he has given me help to fulfill his purpose. As an expression of his love for me, God has opened doors of opportunity that are far greater than I could have ever imagined, in order that I may use the uniqueness of who I am to share the message of Christ. In doing so, God has enabled my pastoral influence to extend in creative ways into my local community and around the world.

My call to ministry is captured well in the words of Paul found in Colossians 3:3–4: "For you died, and your life is now hidden with

Christ in God. When Christ, who is your life, appears, then you also will appear with him in glory." When I came to the point of fully responding to God's call, an amazing thing happened. The life I thought was such a big deal died, and I found myself hidden with Christ in the greater plan of God. Over time I have come to realize that, instead of diminishing my life and dreams, saying yes to God has expanded them, for I traded the smallness of my existence for the vastness of life in God. There is no question that I got the far better end of that deal.

Not long ago, I found myself caught up in an extremely busy season of ministry. Added to the weekly assignments of preaching and teaching, I was involved in mentoring some young men and working with a family to prepare a memorial service for their loved one. Add in some district responsibility and a relational crisis or two in the congregation, and I began to wonder what stress the next phone call or email might bring. All I could do was work my way through each situation and seek to do the next thing faithfully. Sunday came, and I had the privilege once again of standing before a congregation of people for whom I cared deeply and whom I considered my own family. They were willing to call me Pastor—the one they trusted to walk with them through the journey of life, the one they trusted to be God's messenger to proclaim the freeing message of Christ. And somewhere in the midst of that moment, I was reminded again of the call of God on my life, and with a sense of joy, I knew that this is exactly what I was made for. Being a pastor was not something I did to make a living; it was who I was, and I was thankful I said yes to God.

Rev. Simon Jothi
President
South Asia Nazarene Bible College
Bangalore, India

In 1989 at the age of twenty, I served as a volunteer for a mission convention. During the second day of the convention I was listening to the message from outside, and the preacher connected directly to my heart. He said, "I will build my church, and the gates of hades will not prevail." He was talking about the enormous challenges that the apostle Peter faces and how little he understands the highest call from God. Though he denies Jesus, he begins to see what God can accomplish through obedience. Through Peter on the day of Pentecost, thousands of people are added to the kingdom of God. God sees Peter, with his shortcomings and impossibilities, as a valuable worker for the kingdom of God. The preacher said, "If God can use Peter with his limitations, he can use anyone for the extension of his kingdom. God is looking for people who will hear God's call and respond." I was the first one to respond by kneeling down at the altar and committing myself to full-time ministry.

I was disheartened when I talked to my pastor about my call. He did not encourage me and said my education would limit my pursuit of the call. Meanwhile, when all the doors for education were shut, my brother introduced me to a Nazarene pastor. This was the very first time I heard about the Church of the Nazarene. This pastor happily received me and was willing to help me to pursue the call. First, he gave me the Church of the Nazarene's *Manual* so I could understand the doctrine of the Nazarene Church in my mother tongue. I read the *Manual* cover to cover three times. The doctrine of entire sanctification and the polity of the church attracted me. I felt at home when I attended a Nazarene church and was convinced this was where I would like to belong. For the first time I understood the second work of the grace of God. Little did I know that I had previously experienced this grace in Sunday services. These experiences of grace led me into a deeper faith experience.

The church gave me various opportunities to serve and nurtured my call to full-time ministry. For the next two years the church gave me the opportunity to do outreach ministries, and I enjoyed each moment. I saw how God used me as I reached out to people. These first years were not easy because I faced challenges, but God helped me conquer these challenges and formed me for ministry. God showed his power to overcome these challenges and helped me in equipping myself for the practical challenges of ministry.

The church invested in me by sending me to South India Biblical Seminary, one of the Wesleyan Bible schools in India. The seminary focused on academic excellence and spiritual formation, which broadened my understanding of ministry. I maintained a close connection with the local church while I was in seminary by serving in ministry on the weekends. I was able to connect strongly with new believers through my education, and I learned about holiness and Wesleyan theology.

It was hard for me to learn the local language since I was from another state in India. With God's help, I was able to learn the local language in order to communicate, teach, and preach to the people. God reassured me that I can overcome challenges through his mighty power. After my studies, I became a youth pastor in the local church, concentrating on reaching youth and children. I also helped new believers to grow in the Lord through systematic teaching of Scripture. The senior pastor encouraged emerging pastors to engage in church planting, so we developed thirteen individual churches in nearby villages. I encouraged many young people to serve as bivocational pastors and laypeople in these newly established churches. I helped provide basic training to help them actively engage in ministry. As part of the pastoral team, we strengthened each ministry of the church to be an effective transformational agent in the community. The result was spiritual maturity and numerical growth.

The church continued to support my theological studies. I was sent to Union Biblical Seminary, where I developed greater thinking capacities that enabled me to understand Scripture more deeply, which helped me to be more effective in ministry. I initially was a pastor; then, later, I was called to be the registrar for South Asia Nazarene Bible College. Eventually I became the president of the Bible college.

I continue to live out my calling as I see God's faithfulness coming true in my life. The kingdom needs more and more efficient ministers to reach the constantly changing needs of the church, both locally and globally. God still calls men and women for ministry. Your call may be different from my call. It could take place in a variety of ways, in a variety of places. God is able to look beyond the curtains that cover you and shield you from knowing God's plan in your life. Your action of responding to the call of God is a blessing and will be multiplied in many people's lives. There are many amazing people who live their call, and each one faces various challenges, but God shows his mighty power to provide and comfort us. Are you answering God's call in your life?

Rev. Joy Streight
Pastor
Castle Hills Church of the Nazarene
Boise, Idaho

My father was a Nazarene pastor. He loved to move, so our family got acquainted with Idaho and Oregon by living in a variety of parsonages. I joined the family midway through a four-year pastorate in Enterprise, Oregon. Before I was old enough to have any real memories of eastern Oregon, we moved to Marsing, Idaho. When I was almost six, we moved away from conventional pastoring to start a new district campground near Garden Valley, Idaho. We were there just fifteen months, but the sale of the property purchased in 1965 helped make the current Intermountain District Trinity Pines Campground a reality.

Our next home was the parsonage in Jerome, Idaho. One evening, while having my devotions before bedtime, I sensed the Lord calling me to preach. Although I was only nine, I remember flying from my bedroom into my parents' room to excitedly tell them of God's call. They encouraged me, although God's call on my older brother's life was naturally a higher priority since he was soon to head off to college.

Years went by, and it seemed that serving the Lord as a committed layperson would satisfy God's call on my heart. I married a wonderful man, started raising three great children, and continued to serve the church as needed. I taught Bible studies, led worship, and served as a Sunday school superintendent, board member, and choir member. While serving on a district board, I mentioned my call to preach. A pastor on the board immediately urged me to begin the course of study for ordination. I heard her encouragement, but the needs of my family seemed too great to even consider such a thing.

One Sunday our children's pastor announced her resignation. I was surprised by the announcement, and as I sat through the rest of the service, I literally heard the Lord, say, *Now is the time, Joy. Now is the time to answer my call.* I heard the Lord loud and clear, but our congregation had recently gone through a difficult and deep conflict. Subsequently, my husband, who was out of town when this announcement was made, was very protective of me as a leader in the church. I knew he would not think *now* was the time, so I didn't say anything to him about the Lord's audible call that day.

Days later, he came to me and said, "I know this sounds odd coming from me, but I sense the Lord saying that now is the time for you to answer his call." His words shocked me. God was speaking to both of us.

I never had a specific call to children's ministry. I'd been asked before if I would serve in this capacity, but it was never a good time. I went to our new pastor to offer my help, but he didn't know me and graciously declined. I felt an incredible peace knowing I had been obedient to the Lord's call. Surprisingly, within a few weeks, I was the new part-time children's pastor.

I have always loved to work. I thoroughly enjoy interacting with people, solving problems, reaching goals, and meeting people's needs. Customer service was my role in business, and serving as a staff pastor combined my many years of lay ministry with listening to and serving others. I loved it and warned my husband I would never go back to non-ministry employment. That was fine with him, and although it was not easy financially, we made the transition to ministry smoothly and intended to stay in the church we loved for the rest of our days.

However, that was not God's plan. After about six months a dear friend, Dr. Tim Bunn, who pastored just sixteen miles from us, asked me to consider coming to serve his church as children's pastor. My husband quickly voiced his opinion in the negative: It was too far to drive. After many conversations, our friend wisely asked us to pray about it for just three days.

In three days, God uprooted us and made us available to go. After the board approval, tearful goodbyes and a marvelous welcoming, I was a full-time children's pastor in a wonderful nearby community. It was a difficult transition because we had been at our church for a long time—my husband for twenty-four years and me for sixteen. The church we left was truly our family, and it was a significant transition.

After five years, with my ordination study complete, I was ordained as an elder in the Church of the Nazarene. It was a beautiful service and a great milestone, but I had not anticipated the significant and powerful sense of the Holy Spirit's anointing on me that I felt that evening. Soon after, my times of personal devotion and study seemed uncomfortable, and I found myself hurrying through times of personal prayer. God was still calling.

Even now, as I write these words, I sense God's powerful presence. Chills run up and down my spine as I recall the holy discomfort of those days. I knew my call was to preach. I *was* preaching, but my audience members were younger than most congregants. Children's ministry is certainly a call of God, but I knew in my heart that God had called *me* to pastor a church, and I was not answering that call. Two more years passed.

In 2008, during District Assembly, two pastors on our district—one who was pastoring and the other teaching at Northwest Nazarene University—approached me at different times to ask if we could get together soon to talk. I agreed out of friendship and curiosity.

The two appointments ended up being set for the same day, just a week away. The first was with Dr. Rhonda Carrim at NNU. She asked me where I saw myself serving the Lord in five years.

I answered, perhaps a bit too quickly, "I just want to be faithful, wherever God has me."

She pushed a bit further. "If there were no barriers, no reasons not to, where would God have you serve?"

I answered a bit tentatively, "I would be pastoring a church somewhere."

She answered with a single word: "Bingo!"

We laughed together, and then the conversation that followed was my long list of reasons why I would probably never realize this dream. One of the major factors was that I had completed my ordination study through NNU, but since we were on a shoestring financial budget in those days, I paid audit fees and only completed the work necessary to qualify for ordination. Without an undergraduate degree, no church would hire me. Another factor was that, at that time, the only female pastors on our district were staff pastors, not lead pastors, and one was a co-pastor with her husband. No solo-female lead pastors. So it simply was not possible.

After my meeting with Dr. Carrim, I went to my second appointment for that day, with Pastor Mark Harmon, from Lakeview Church of the Nazarene. His opening words to me were, "Where do you see yourself serving the Lord in five years?"

I laughed and asked him if he had been conspiring with Dr. Carrim from NNU, but he said he had not. God was with all of us. I quickly told him what I had told Dr. Carrim that morning.

He didn't seem daunted by the seeming impossibilities. He challenged me to trust the reality of my call to preach. He also encouraged me to tell our district superintendent, Dr. Stephen Borger, about my call.

I voiced my concern over taking up Dr. Borger's precious time over something so small. Dr. Harmon assured me Dr. Borger would want to know.

I ended up trusting Dr. Harmon and having that time-consuming conversation with Dr. Borger, telling him I knew I needed to complete my education before I would be truly eligible to serve as lead pastor anywhere. He leaned across the table and assured me that I was already qualified in the eyes of the denomination but that the consideration of *any* candidate was up to church boards. We prayed together, and I submitted my résumé. Three months later, a church called. Two months after we interviewed, the church asked me to be their pastor.

Six months after that beginning, our congregation merged with a second to form a new church, Castle Hills Church of the Nazarene. This new congregation then voted on its pastor. There were so many reasons for them to be uncertain, reluctant, or even opposed, but God came near, and the people voted unanimously.

God called me as a nine-year-old, and forty years later God's church and I fully embraced the call to preach and pastor. Now, through the generosity of my husband's parents, I am completing my education. God is not daunted by age or gender. God is not troubled by impossible situations, and God's call transcends our expectations and dreams. God is faithful; praise his name!

Rev. Jay and Rev. Teanna Sunberg
Missionaries
Church of the Nazarene
Budapest, Hungary

Teanna's Story

How did I get here? I am sitting on the corner of Október 6 and Zrínyi Street on one of Budapest's first sunny days of the spring season. There are languages all around me, pedestrians from a plethora of countries, tourists, businesspeople, and local Hungarians. But this is a question of a different nature. Remove the church lens that celebrates missions, and the question could have a foreboding tone: "What are you doing here?"

My story begins with four syllables: mis-sion-ar-y. I have a working hypothesis that there is a vocabulary list full of familiar words that in actuality have very fluid meanings. Missionary is such a word. Push past the first sentence that describes it, and you arrive at a lot of um, well, you know, scratch the head and shift to the other foot. Or "a missionary is someone who goes to another country and tells people about Jesus." Eventually, you arrive at *evangelize, convert, preach,* and all of it depicted within the setting of an impoverished, homogenous Africa replete with backward villages, starving children with bloated bellies, and the complimentary buzzing fly for effect. Or an illegal house church in the heart of China. Or a boat in the Amazon.

Those were my ideas when the Lord whispered *missions* into my ear at the age of fourteen. I was a new believer who had barely wrapped my mind around Jesus living in my heart when, suddenly, I was packing my bags to wave a comfortable future and the American dream goodbye.

"No!" I said it loudly enough to be heard over the Christian band rocking the concert. I said it loudly enough so the African kid on the projector screen could hear me over the buzzing fly. I said it loudly

and strongly enough to shut God up and move him into safer territory. Sometimes, though, God can be annoyingly stubborn.

For several months God bothered me with this ridiculous idea of
missions. I had no concept of what missionaries really did with their
time, but I was convinced their duties held absolutely no interest for
me.

Eventually, it occurred to me that my repetitive no might be a bit
unseemly for someone who had newly promised to follow Jesus. I had
somehow acquired the notion that God and I were supposed to be
heading in the same direction, and if we were not, one of us was required to quickly correct course. Since God continued to pester me,
and I was undoubtedly set against the bad idea of missions, I found
myself in the middle of a genius prayer.

"Lord," I said, with a sneaky grin, "Missions is a terrible idea for me.
I don't like it. I don't want it. I cannot say yes, but I'm trying my best
to get to heaven here. I'm trying to be a Christian here. So, if you want
me to be a missionary, you will have to change my heart. Amen." I was
only fourteen years old, and quite honestly I did not hear another word
from God about missions until I was twenty-five. God was silent on the
subject for eleven years, but I was learning to speak.

At the ripe old age of fifteen, during the fall of my sophomore
year of high school, freshly saved, I stared at my class schedule and a
list of electives. Not particularly enamored of any category of math
or science, I scribbled Spanish onto the form and reported to Mrs.
Good's *Española* classroom. There were piñatas dancing from the
ceiling and decidedly Latin American decorations everywhere.

Mrs. Good had been born just a few years late for Woodstock,
but that had not prevented her from adopting a splendidly Bohemian
lifestyle. While most of her contemporaries went to college to become part of corporate America, Mrs. Good had wafted through her
twenties in exploration of 1970s Europe. She lived with a German
family in Bavaria, hitchhiked through Spain, and sipped the wines

of France. Eventually she returned to set up house in a common-law marriage with an organic farmer in my Kansas community. She wasn't particularly fond of religion, except as an art form, but the woman had stories—fascinating stories of culture and people and language and scenery.

In my third year of high school, I was faced with more electives in my schedule, so I took Spanish II and German I. In my last year of high school, Mrs. Good decided to teach French for the first time, and together we journeyed each afternoon through Spanish III, German II, and French I. Somewhere during the unit on Madrid, right around reflexive verb tenses, I realized that, more than anything in the world, I wanted to experience Europe. I wanted to travel, but not as a tourist who merely checks sights off a list—I wanted to know people and their culture, language, and world. I had a dream, and absolutely no idea how God was going to make my dream come true.

At the age of eighteen, I went to MidAmerica Nazarene University and managed to skip every Nazarene missions service over the course of the next seven years because missions seemed boring. When Jay and I met and fell in love as students at MidAmerica, traveling became a discussion. I was honest about my desire to experience Europe and to do it before we had children.

Jay's Story

All I ever wanted when I grew up was to be like my father, who was a pastor. Growing up in a Nazarene parsonage was a good thing. I loved it. My father had a unique combination of attributes—physically big and strong, yet generous, gentle, and compassionate in his interactions with people. I wanted to be just like him. I wanted to be a pastor.

One weekend, a missionary came to our home. I really don't remember much about him except that he was a medical missionary from Africa. I do clearly recall that he teased me all weekend by calling me "gourd head," a name I did not appreciate. Though I was intrigued by his display table, I cannot recall much from the services except feeling a strong pull inside that I did not understand. Following the service I spoke with my mother, who was the most influential person in my spiritual life. She helped me understand that God was calling me to ministry. I was excited about that call.

The next Sunday evening, my father asked me to give a testimony in church about what had happened in the missions service. Dutifully, I stood and declared that I felt God calling me to ministry. People in the church were supportive but began to ask me to what I felt God was calling me. I did not know, but since the missionary had been in medical missions, I said, "I am called to medical missions." Honestly, I was disappointed with this answer. It may not sound like a big difference, but for me, medical missions was not pastoring. I wanted to be a pastor like my father, and I struggled with what I thought was my call throughout my entire high school career. When asked, I would say that I was called to medical missions but that my heart's desire was to be a pastor.

When I enrolled at MidAmerica Nazarene College (now University), I was forced to make decisions about my major. There was a clear direction in ministry. In speaking to my advisor regarding my dilemma, he advised me to take general education classes first and think about it for a semester. As a freshman I was paired with a roommate I actually knew from our Bible quizzing days—we were rivals from different districts. We became good friends and remain so today. Interestingly, Mark was a pre-med major and I remember the afternoon he bought his textbooks. I took a look at those tomes and had absolutely no interest in what he was studying. That revelation made it easier to make the decision to focus my study in the department of religion. With my trajectory set, I felt relieved, yet I still worried that perhaps I was not completely listening to God.

As my academic direction progressed, God brought my life into contact with Teanna. We began to share our dreams with each other. I imagined I would pastor a small church and learn how to pastor effectively. I envisioned my pastoral experiences molding me into a pastor who birthed new churches, and I was excited about seeing my dreams come to fruition. Teanna dreamed of traveling and experiencing Europe before we had children. But how could that happen on a young pastor's salary? I wondered how God would ever make that work.

After graduating from college, I entered seminary. We were newly married, and I was working toward my dream. I had just said goodbye to my brother and his family, who moved to Moscow, Russia, to be pioneer missionaries in the wake of the fall of the Berlin Wall. As they settled into a new reality, our family was excited to hear new information of their Russian adventures. Eighteen months into their experience in Moscow, my brother came home for Nazarene General Assembly. I volunteered to pick them up at the airport, eager to get those first stories. I will never forget the first words my brother said to me: "I want to talk to you about your future."

Our Story

And that is how we found ourselves on a Boeing 747, en route to the former Soviet Union's capital city of Moscow, Russia. We were twenty-six years old and three months out of seminary. Our first pastoral appointment was a short-term missionary contract to pastor the first and only Nazarene church in Moscow. We faced the learning curve of all learning curves.

God has quite a sense of humor. Teanna got her Europe experience. Jay got his heart's desire to pastor. But it looked much different than either of us ever dreamed. Two years later, we had gone through the process of becoming contracted missionaries. It was a commitment we did not take lightly. It was a call that had its origins in our childhoods, but the confirmation and passion of its reality was realized when God grafted us into the soil of Eastern Europe.

After four years in Moscow, we moved to Sofia, Bulgaria, where we had the joy of living for thirteen years. Today we live in Budapest, Hungary, and are attempting to learn our third language about a beautiful culture. Perhaps, in all honesty, we are no closer to answering that evasive question of what a missionary is or does. God's call comes for some in a moment and for others through a process of revelation. When God calls, God makes a way, and the call to serve as a missionary is distinct, definite, and life changing.

So perhaps the question on the corner still remains unanswered. What are we doing here? We are simply living our lives and watching for every opportunity to fall in step with Jesus and what he is doing in our world.

Rev. Ruben Villarreal
Pastor
ThornCreek Church of the Nazarene
Thornton, Colorado

"Paul, a bond-servant of Christ Jesus, called as an apostle, set apart for the gospel of God" (Romans 1:1, NASB). God gave me this verse when I was on vacation in the Bahamas with my family. We were on a small island known as Spanish Wells. I was swimming in the ocean with my daughter, and I was standing about chest high in the water. However, my daughter was not able to reach the bottom, so I held her with both arms. I realized how scary the ocean can appear. On one side you could see land, and on the other side you could only see raging waters. You don't know what's below the surface and the deeper you go, the more unknowns there are. At that point I saw the fear in my daughter's eyes. She yelled, "Don't let me go, Daddy, don't let me go!"

My first thought was, *How absurd that my daughter is even thinking I would let her go.* My second thought was, *She doesn't realize how much I love her.*

Just after that second thought, I heard God tell me, *Ruben, I have you, and I love you; why are you afraid?* Then God immediately reminded me of Romans 1:1. At this point the calling of God on my life went to another level.

The calling of God is romantic. There is something romantic about packing your belongings, pronouncing to the world that you are going into ministry, and proceeding down the unknown road with unlimited possibilities. Will you be the next Andy Stanley, Craig Groeschel, or Steven Furtick? Why not? You are ready to take on hell with a squirt gun! You are full of bridled ideas, and you can finally unleash them and shock the world.

To be honest, those thoughts crossed my mind in the early days of my calling. I am grateful that God gives space and grace to work through our callings. I was slow in responding to God's call in my life. However, it became secure at Nazarene Youth Congress (now Conference) in 1987. Tony Campolo was preaching a message at the University of Maryland stadium. I walked down many steps and knelt at a makeshift altar (God does his best work at altars). I dropped my net and invited God's Holy Spirit to lead me. Because of that decision, I am here today.

The calling of God is a journey about who you are and about who God is. It is the same call Jesus gives the first disciples. It is the charge to drop your net and follow him. Initially, that charge is about things we can understand such as go to school for ministry preparation, go this route, take these courses, and complete these assignments. However, a true calling of God takes you increasingly deeper into the core of your will.

You may not be called by God to be a pastor, and that is okay! God will use you! Identifying with a phrase of your favorite chorus does not necessarily mean God is calling you. Getting "God chills" during a message does not mean God is calling you to move to Chile! The fact that your parents or grandparents were pastors or missionaries does not necessarily mean God is calling you to do the same. Just because your attention is drawn to a LeBron James billboard that says "Witness," that does not mean God is calling you. When I hear about people feeling called by Christ to serve him in ministry, I tell them to run. If you are miserable and a black cloud covers your head, then go down the road of pursuing that call.

The calling of God will *always* be affirmed by the spiritual leadership God has put in your life. I had several pastors who affirmed God's calling on my life. Additionally, God made it clear to me repeatedly through Scripture. God will use people who understand the calling of God to affirm that the calling is legitimately *from* God. Never ignore the spiritual wisdom of those whom God has placed above you, and never make a calling from God a selfish pursuit.

When God showed me Romans 1:1, it rocked my world. God reminded me that I am his bond servant and apostle. It reminded me that I have been set apart for the gospel. It is not something I chose; it is a response. I tell people all the time, "I have no life, but I have an amazing life." A true calling of God compels you to love everything less, including hometown, parents, and the familiar. It's not a calling that says, *I will go anywhere as long as it's within three hours of home.* It's a surrendered heart that says, *I'll go anywhere God wants me to go, and I will leave everything because I know God will sustain me.* It is a calling that grabs your lifelong desires and goals and realigns them with a kingdom purpose. This holy alignment will jostle you, grind your will, and bring you to the place of brokenness. It is a calling to lose your identity in Christ Jesus, die to your grand ambitions, and be willing to sweep the floor for the kingdom of God.

The calling of God involves hurt. Jesus said he did not entrust himself to the heart of people because he knew their human nature. I do not think anyone would argue that Jesus loved people, or was obedient to his calling. But for those who are called it means a willingness to be hurt by those who eat at your table, a church board member, or even a staff member. In the midst of these hurts you will still remain faithful to the calling of God by loving and forgiving these people.

The calling of God can be un-anointed. You can go through the motions of ministry and use your gifts and strengths and not be anointed by God's Spirit. The calling and the anointing are two different works of the Spirit. Obtaining the anointing requires faithfulness when nobody is looking. Following a call is something everyone can see. But you need both. God will entrust you with greater measures of the work of his Holy Spirit as you surrender these corners of your life. There's no way around it. Go big or go home!

At ThornCreek Church, we have been blessed to see much growth. When you have an increase in numbers you get a lot of attention. However, the truth is that some of the greatest pastors out there are in churches with no growth. Incidentally, some of the most influential leaders for the kingdom of God came from churches of under 150. Many of these are bivocational pastors who serve with little applause. They are my heroes. Never let the size of your ministry determine the size of your faithfulness. When you are faithful with little, God will entrust you with more, and more does not necessarily mean a bigger church. The privilege of the calling is that you are used by God. That is the honor.

The truth is that the call of God is irrevocable. I have been in full-time ministry for more than twenty years. I started ThornCreek Church of the Nazarene thirteen years ago in my living room. During this time I have seen colleagues who were called to ministry walk away. All had great dreams at one point. All had a genuine love for God. Today, cities are full of salespeople, insurance agents, Realtors, plumbers, construction people, teachers, para-church employees, and Christian camp employees who have a calling from God in their lives and who have walked away from those callings. Perhaps it was sin, personal ambition, or a host of other reasons. What I have discovered is that a true calling from God will make your life miserable until you obey that call. It is also possible for you to intentionally set aside your calling. Eventually, God will let you have your way. God will still be with you because God loves you. But you will miss out on a much richer life.

The calling of God is like an ocean. It is like looking out into that ocean and not being able to feel the bottom but being comfortable with it. You will encounter sharks, jellyfish, dangerous reefs, and other garbage, but God is with you. God will show you the depth of his grace, love, and redemptive plan. God will constantly remind you that he loves you and is holding you. You will also gain a keen awareness that it is not about you!

6 Emeritus Leader Narratives

Emeritus leaders are ministers of the gospel who have retired from full-time ministry but who are still actively fulfilling their calling. The word *emeritus* in the context of ministry often refers to people who have held a particular office or role in the church but who are now engaged in a different kind of ministry. These leaders have followed God's call throughout their lives, and that call continues to thrust them into new avenues of ministry today. These emeritus leaders have a wealth of experience, knowledge, and wisdom in life and in their calling as ministers of the gospel. As you read these stories, we trust you will see how these leaders have given their lives to the church and to the kingdom and how their love for Jesus and the church captures their hearts and minds. We have much to learn from these saints.

Rev. Dave and Rev. Carolita Fraley
Former Missionaries to France and Current Pastors
Canyon Hill Church of the Nazarene
Caldwell, Idaho

Our call to missions is really a story of God's faithfulness and everlasting love. At every turn God was there. Our loving heavenly Father took care of us by supplying our spiritual, physical, and emotional needs. He should receive all the praise for all that has happened in our lives.

Carolita's Story

I come from a large family. The two youngest sisters are the only ones under six feet tall. In fact, at one time, we were named the tallest family in Seattle, with oversized hearts too. Anyone who walked into the Seattle Highland Park Church of the Nazarene looking even a little bit alone would be scooped up into our family circle and taken home for dinner. You should plan on spending the night—or the week, if necessary.

My dad, Ed Freeman, walked the same mail route for forty years. Using his Bible school training, he shared whatever he could—a word of encouragement, a friendly smile, or an invitation to church. He was also known as the man with the golden musical saw. Irene, my mom, was an ordained deaconess who gave daily lessons to us on how to become the greatest of all in God's kingdom. She was a servant to everyone, often sharing whatever our family had.

The summer of my thirteenth year, while attending teen camp, I had my first indication that God wanted me to be a missionary. During an altar service, I said yes to a call, thinking God was only testing me. Several days later, I did stand up on a Sunday evening at my home church and testify that God had definitely spoken to me.

Dave's Story

I was born, the second of four children, into a Christian home similar to Carolita's. My parents, Earl and Jane, were devoted to God, their church, and their children. Our home was open to others, and there were many memories of sitting around the dining room table Sunday noon, surrounded by friends. My dad was in the Navy, so moving was a part of our family life.

At a very early age I gave my heart to the Lord, and, as many kids do, I went to the altar often to confirm that decision. At age thirteen, in Long Beach, California, I stood up during a Sunday evening testimony time. Before I realized what I was saying, I told everyone that God had called me to be a medical missionary. I have no conscious recollection of ever considering missionary service before that time.

Our Story Begins

We met at Northwest Nazarene College (now NNU) on a blind date, during which we learned that we had both been called to missionary service. In God's way of doing things, we found ourselves sitting next to each other in assigned chapel seats at the start of school that next fall term. After a few months of growing friendship, we had our first official date and, prophetically, went to hear missionaries to Taiwan Donna and George Rench.

Separation was the next step in our relationship as Dave left NNC to continue his schooling at California State University in Long Beach. Questions came about his call to be a missionary doctor. Would he have the good grades he needed to get into medical school? Outside of the great relationship with Carolita, there was a lack of certainty about his future.

Carolita spent the next year at NNC and graduated with a degree in elementary education. Soon after, she moved to southern California, where she had signed a teaching contract. But, the summer of her arrival, Dave left for Texas for Peace Corps training. After returning to Long Beach in August, on the night before his departure to Africa for two years, Dave asked Carolita to marry him and to wait for his return. She said yes, and he left for Morocco the next day. We were sure of our love for each other, but there were many questions about how our call would work out.

In looking back at that time in our lives, it is easy to see that God had many things to teach us. We learned about the durability of our love as a couple, as two years of separation only drew us closer together. Dave was able to learn French as well as how to adapt to a foreign environment. We were married soon after Dave came back to the States.

With many questions about our future still unanswered, one thing remained certain: We would serve God, even though the how and where still needed to be worked out. It would take another ten years before those answers came.

Dave went back to school again, still studying to be a doctor, but that attempt was not successful. Carolita worked part-time on several jobs, but when Dave became subject to the military draft, he signed up for air traffic control school with the Navy. Carolita continued to teach while Dave served active duty.

There soon came a change in our perspective. Perhaps it was time to drop the idea of *medical* missions. When Dave returned to school as a psychology major, there was immediate academic success and a great sense of fulfillment and relief. Dave graduated from college in 1973.

The Next Steps

We settled into our married life together. Carolita quit her teaching career. Dave found a job as a manager and buyer for a clothing store owned by people in the church. A few months later, we were expecting our first child. Our life was comfortable, our ministry in the Long Beach Church of the Nazarene had been established, and our first son was born.

However, it soon became evident that something was lacking. There was an uneasy feeling, something empty in our lives. It was a sure thing that our call to missions was still there. We profited from every opportunity to be with missionaries. As the months went by, the burning became stronger and stronger. Times of prayer about our calling increased.

Finally, there was an event that rocked our world. After a young adult missionary meeting at our church, each of us brought home a missionary book to read. We had two copies of the same book, *New Strategies for Missions*. The second chapter was about France as a future mission field for the Church of the Nazarene. As we read the book together, God spoke to us as a couple, breaking our hearts for the immense spiritual needs of the French. We immediately prayed together and then called another couple in our church and asked them to pray for us. We asked specifically for a sign that God was talking to us about France.

Five days later, we arrived at church to find that Steve Weber, a newly assigned missionary to Haiti, had called our pastor during the week to see if he could come and speak on Sunday. As he stood at the pulpit, he talked about how he should be speaking about his new area of work in Haiti but that God had put in his heart the desire to speak about the spiritual needs of the country where he had just finished his language training, France. We were amazed by this change of events. At the end of the presentation, Steve said he believed there could be a young couple in the service that morning who were considering going to France as missionaries. Would that couple come down and pray with him? We got up immediately and went to the altar. After a time of prayer with Steve, we decided it was time to call our church headquarters and apply to be sent as missionaries. The process began with a preliminary application. There was an interview in San Diego, a second, more detailed application, and, eventually, an invitation to come to Kansas City to attend Nazarene Theological Seminary (NTS). We made the decision to move to Kansas City in time for the spring semester.

We had no money, but we had reached a decision that if God was in this, God would provide a way to get there. We reserved a U-Haul truck to move our household items, knowing there was no money to pay the $500 fee. Carolita's parents offered to help us drive the truck and our car, and pay for gas. On our last Sunday night at church, we were sent off to Kansas City with a love offering. A total of $503 was given to us, enabling us to pay the deposit with enough left over for a couple cups of coffee.

After four days on the road, we arrived in Kansas City. The temperature in Long Beach was 80 degrees and in Kansas City it was –20. We had $12 in our pocket, no place to live, no job, Carolita was eight weeks pregnant, and Dave had not yet been accepted to NTS. Carolita's sister had just moved to Kansas City, so we did have a place to land. In the next three days God gave Dave a part-time job, a place to live, acceptance to NTS, and some money in the bank. We began to see God at work in very practical ways.

God's Provision

There are too many things we could share about how God met our needs during our two-year stay in Kansas City. Here are some of the highlights:

- During our first Sunday, we visited the Shawnee Church of the Nazarene, a place that eventually became a second family and supported us in prayer and friendships.
- Our monthly income from Dave's part-time job could pay many of our bills but left nothing for food. A small prayer group in California sent us a weekly check that put something on our table ($35-a-week food budget).

- Carolita needed some dental care at the UMKC dental school. Every time she went, the Lord provided extra money to pay for the work.
- Our second son, Mark, was born in September, but we had no insurance. Dave's dad sent money for the hospital bill, but the doctor's bill was $500. A friend from the Shawnee church learned that we had a stamp collection for sale. He offered us $500. When the doctor's bill was $50 more than planned, our stamp-buying friend voluntarily gave us 50 extra dollars without knowing about the additional cost.
- After our first year in Kansas City, we wrote a Christmas letter to our family, friends, and home church. The envelopes sat on our table for a couple of days because there was no money for stamps. The next day in the mail, we received from a friend in Long Beach a letter that contained two sheets of stamps— enough to send our letters out. That friend had no idea what our need was.

In looking back at this time in Kansas City, we realize that God was getting us ready for thirty years of missionary service, where we would monthly spend 90 percent of our salary at the grocery store in order to feed three hungry boys and keep them in tennis shoes. We never felt poor or neglected. God gave us everything we ever needed, just as he promises in Matthew 6:25–33.

The Call Continues

After almost thirty years in France, we returned home to Nampa, Idaho, in 2008. The following year, we became pastors of the Canyon Hill Church of the Nazarene in Caldwell, Idaho, where we still serve today. God has been faithful, and continues to be faithful, to our call to be missionaries.

Rev. Dr. Nina Griggs Gunter
General Superintendent Emeritus
Church of the Nazarene
Nashville, Tennessee

God loves small things. Jesus says the kingdom of God is like a mustard seed, like a little bit of yeast, like a pearl, like finding a lost coin, like one lost sheep, like five loaves and two fish. The kingdom belongs to little children. Zechariah 4:10 encourages us not to despise small things. In verse 6 God declares: "Not by might, nor by power, but by my spirit."

Answering the Call

I was humbled to discover that God calls the unimpressive, the least of these—even a farm girl from Wallace, South Carolina. I sensed that God was talking to me about ministry at a rather young age. My constant exposure to pastors, evangelists, district superintendents, and missionaries made me more aware of God's Spirit. My parents' leading of our daily family devotions influenced my sensitivity to God's call. I loved to listen to preachers, even as a small child. Though I enjoyed the music in church, I was eager for it to finish so I could hear the preacher. My analytical mind followed the sermons, outlined the Scriptures, and noted key thoughts in the story.

When I was twelve years old, I one day became very burdened during my devotions and wondered what God was saying to me. I began to pray, "God, I will do anything you ask me to do—just help me to be sure." As I began to read the Bible while still on my knees, God affirmed to me with crystal clarity: *Minister before the Lord* (see 1 Samuel 2:18). The burden lifted, and peace flooded my soul.

Later, at the age of fourteen, I made an entire devotion to God to honor and glorify him in response to his call to ministry. From that small but significant beginning, that call has stayed constant in purpose and service.

Fulfilling the Call

During my years at Trevecca Nazarene University, Dwight Moody Gunter and I were married and began our ministries of preaching and co-pastoring. We soon realized we needed to supplement our income, and God had prepared me to meet this financial need. In addition to a bachelor's degree in religion, I had a degree in education and a master's degree in counseling. This background allowed me to be employed as a high school guidance counselor in the community where we pastored. God taught me in those days that ministry need not be compartmentalized. In that local context, the opportunity to serve the one and only public high school in a community of 15,000 resulted in an incredible introduction of our church and, more importantly, a Christian influence in the lives of teachers, students, and their families. Some persons from those relationships are in ministry today.

After eighteen years of co-pastoring, God opened new avenues of ministry for both of us. Moody served as district superintendent and, later, finance director for the Church of the Nazarene. I became the global director of Nazarene Missions International (NMI) and, later, was elected general superintendent of the Church of the Nazarene.

The preaching ministry remained paramount, and I often preached at district and international NMI conventions, regional conferences, and local church Faith Promise services. There continue to be numerous opportunities for me to preach at revivals, camp meetings, retreats, and school commencements. While serving as general superintendent in the Church of the Nazarene, there were hundreds of international district assemblies at which to preach, preside, and ordain.

Inclusivity of the Call

Along the way, the avenues for ministry, which include the message of the gospel for inclusivity, have been evident. God validates his call in our lives to meet the needs of an ever-changing global community.

South Korea

As I prepared to travel to South Korea to preach, preside over, and ordain at District Assembly, the district superintendent contacted me to pass on a request from the evangelical television station in Seoul to film my preaching and do an interview. Since no female leader of a denomination had ever ministered in South Korea in leading a legislative meeting of a denomination and ordaining ministers as elders, the television network wanted to broadcast the news and the service across South Korea. I was pleased to think this would honor God and the church.

Papua New Guinea

When I arrived in the Highlands area near Kudjip, the district superintendent of the Western Highlands District (the mother district of the fourteen districts in Papua New Guinea), I began to walk through the proposed agenda of District Assembly. When we came to the report of the Ministerial Credentials committee, the district superintendent paused. Then he proceeded to tell me that, for the first time in the district's fifty-three-year history, the committee had voted to recommend the ordination of three women as elders.

Later, when we came to this item of business in the assembly, with hundreds of delegates present, I carefully and openly presented the report of the committee. Even though I gave them the opportunity to ask questions, there were none, and the vote was unanimous. There was an obvious sacredness and an indescribable celebration in the ordination service that evening with the more than one thousand people in attendance. These three God-called women, who had been waiting for years with patience, expectation, and obedience to God's call, were ordained as Nazarene elders in the church of God. Since then, many more women across PNG have been ordained. God still calls!

Japan

In my first visit to Japan, I wasn't sure about cultural responses, but I was confident of everyone's relationship with Jesus Christ. It was the celebration of the district's centennial of the Church of the Nazarene in Japan. The business agenda also called for the election of a new district superintendent. The district leaders were gracious enough to invite me to bring the keynote address in the centennial celebration service and to be the commencement speaker for the seminary graduation. They accommodated me graciously as I presided and preached in the various services, including the ordination service, and in the election of a new district superintendent.

The balloting began for the election. Much to my surprise, on the sixth ballot, the delegates elected a woman to lead the Japan District. She was the first woman to be elected district superintendent in Japan and in all the Asia-Pacific Region. There was a spirit of celebratory worship and recognition of God's call.

Continuing the Call in Retirement

A person in retirement can be a significant resource. My ministry opportunities have shifted, but the opportunity to serve continues. God has gifted me with valuable life experiences in the past that stretch my leadership skills and wisdom into retirement. All of those blessings are given for kingdom purposes.

In the biblical story of Jesus feeding the five thousand with five loaves and two fish (Matthew 14:15–21), have you noticed when the miracle happens? It is not when the little boy gives his lunch to Jesus; it is not when Jesus looks up and asks the Father to bless the lunch; it is not when Jesus gives the small lunch to the disciples. The miracle happens when the disciples begin to give to others the small pieces of the lunch that Jesus has given to them.

God still calls women and men to give to others the gift he has given to us. Then everyone will be filled. First Corinthians 1:26 says to think of what you were when you were called. Not many are wise by human standards or influential or of noble birth. Yes, God calls the least of these. For God loves small things.

Rev. Jerry Hull
Pastor and Professor Emeritus of Social Work
Northwest Nazarene University
Nampa, Idaho

An alfalfa farm eighteen miles out of Weiser, Idaho, provided summer employment in 1954 for me. One hot July day, I reworked a stack of baled hay so we could add several more layers of bales. An anticipated ordinary and mundane morning became extraordinary. God invaded my space and mind and spirit. The encounter that July morning has shaped all of my subsequent choices and life decisions. God spoke in tones louder than words and invited me to ministry. I had turned sixteen three months earlier and could not envision the multiplied dimensions and nuances and characteristics of a call to ministry. Sixty-one years later, some of the contours of the call are more apparent as the learning curve continues.

How do I live out my call now, as I celebrate birthday number seventy-seven? Each morning we may anticipate delight and joy in the Lord. One prayer from Psalm 25 helps launch my day: "Show me your ways, LORD, teach me your paths. Guide me in your truth and teach me, for you are God my Savior, and my hope is in you all day long. Remember, LORD, your great mercy and love, for they are from of old" (Psalm 25:4–6).

Given my life's passions and experiences, my attention is focused on five tasks in my eighth decade:

1. Pray: Praying describes an important option for older persons committed to spirituality. Daily I pray for family members, church leaders, an odd collection of acquaintances and former colleagues, international figures such as Pope Francis and President Obama, leaders of my denomination, and leaders at Northwest Nazarene University. Recently I spent a year reflecting on the nature of prayer and the how-to of prayer. In

this process, I developed sixty short essays on prayer that I hope will assist others to enjoy prayer and have confidence in the One to whom we pray.

2. Encourage: Across the years I have shared thousands of notes and emails and phone messages meant to encourage. Other people are a joy, and I love to connect and interact with them. For example, each week, I focus in prayer on ten current employees of NNU (my young colleagues). At the end of that week, I send words of appreciation and blessing to each of them.

3. Write: My love affair with words began in the third grade at Conklin Elementary school. The teacher assigned me to write a few words about the importance of the Nile River in Egypt. Up to that time I knew about the Snake, Malheur, and Payette Rivers, but learning about the Nile River introduced me to a world beyond fifty miles from my house. My awareness of the world has been expanding ever since.

During childhood, my career interests included word-focused endeavors such as being an auctioneer or a journalist or a preacher. My career in ministry was first logged in local congregations demanding teaching, preaching, counseling, and supervising leadership teams, which tasks required thousands of words. The local parish context consumed my life for ten years.

A second venue for ministry occurred within two regional colleges and universities for the Church of the Nazarene. In the college setting, I met with classes of students each week. In the classroom we employed words to share ideas, worldviews, dreams, and passions with young hearts and minds sorting through callings and career options. Teaching and college administrative tasks comprised decades of my life. I employed thousands of words to write policies, lectures, examinations, and accreditation reports. In addition, I read a huge, unknown tally of tests and term papers and reports. My love affair with words continues to deepen. The first day after retirement from full-time work (2007), I projected a daily writing schedule. Each day begins with one to two hours of study and writing on Christian devotional topics.

4. Volunteer: This area requires extra vigilance for old folks, who battle with with travels, medical appointments, caregiving and erratic energy levels to complicate our days. Social engagement is vital for old folks, and volunteering permits connections with others and offers important areas for service and ministry. For more than thirty years, I have found a good niche in local corps programs of the Salvation Army. The Salvation Army programs provide a good theological match and a structure where I may participate as a minister, sociologist, and social worker. Leadership tasks and facilitating services for the poor and at-risk have dominated my volunteering with the Salvation Army.

5. Give Care: Connections within family, friendship networks, and congregations provide links for caregiving. Sometimes we extend care, and sometimes we receive care. We need skills and competence for both.

I have identified five dimensions for how I understand God's desires for me as I continue to live out my call. Elderly years are full of the unexpected. Often interruptions occur. Regardless, how do we persist in fulfilling a calling throughout an entire lifetime? The words of Psalm 25 offer fresh perspective for each new day. "In you, LORD my God, I put my trust" (v. 1). The prayer concludes with a confident declaration: "May integrity and uprightness protect me, because my hope, LORD, is in you" (v. 21). Enclosed between these verses are instructions for seeking God and God's wisdom for each new day. The passage has become my daily prayer for guidance. The God honored in this prayer has been sufficient from age sixteen through today, and God will be my all in all through decade eight and beyond.

Rev. Bob Luhn
Retired Pastor
Othello Church of the Nazarene
Othello, Washington

I grew up in a loving, Nazarene family in Spokane, Washington, and I consider myself to be incredibly blessed by my heritage. I went to Northwest Nazarene University in 1966 after having never accepted Christ as my Savior. I enrolled as a chemistry major, planning a long career working in a lab. It seemed like a perfect fit for a shy introvert like me.

In January of 1967, less than halfway through my freshman year, the girl I was dating at the time asked me, "Bob, are you a Christian? I never hear you talk about God."

I told her, "No, I'm not a Christian. I've always wanted to be one but could never figure out how to do it."

We ended up over at my basketball coach's house. Elmore Vail was a Christian I admired. I had eaten in his home, and I knew I would be welcomed. I knocked on his door, and when he answered, I said, "Coach, I want to become a Christian." He led me through several scriptures, and then I knelt in his living room, confessed my sins, begged God's forgiveness, and invited Jesus to rule my life.

I honestly didn't feel any different after this prayer. In fact, within a half hour, I became rather angry with God. As I jogged angrily around the campus, I ended up shaking my fist at God, saying, "I don't care whether you accept me. I'm going to be a Christian whether you like it or not!" For the next thirty-six hours I read my Bible, prayed, even witnessed to people, still madder than hops at God because I didn't feel forgiven or at peace or joyful or loving. None of the things promised by the gospel seemed true. Still, I was determined to be a Christian whether God liked it or not.

On Friday morning, January 27, 1967, during breakfast, a wave of love washed over me so powerfully that I knew beyond a shadow of a doubt that I was loved, accepted, and forgiven by God. I often wondered why God let me wallow in anger for those thirty-six hours. I came to believe it was because God wanted my will above all. His call upon my life would lead me into some dark and difficult days, in which the only thing that would keep me going was the will to follow him, whether he liked it or not—and whether I liked it or not.

Over the next several months, I grew spiritually by leaps and bounds, was filled with the Holy Spirit in April of 1967, and became passionate about sharing my faith. My interest in chemistry dried up completely, and my interest in Christ grew exponentially. Since I lacked a clear sense of direction, I spent my sophomore year of college as an undeclared major. I just took general courses that would be foundational for any major. I did receive a prophetic word during that year: *"You are my chosen vessel; walk one step at a time."* I didn't see that as a call to ministry, but I certainly treasured it in my heart.

In the spring of 1968, NNU announced the formation of a new major called Philosophy and Religion. The moment that announcement was made in chapel, I knew in my heart that was what God wanted me to do. I signed up for the required courses and ended up graduating a term early. After graduation, I attended Nazarene Theological Seminary. My experience was educationally satisfying, but it was a spiritual desert for me. Again, I felt like I was only able to go on sheer willpower. There were no consolations from the Lord, no sense of his presence, love, or joy in my life.

By my senior year, I was scared. I remember pouring out my heart to the Lord, "Jesus, in a few short months I'll graduate and take a church. I'll be expected to preach the good news, but honestly, there's no good news in my life." I was studying hard at seminary, working far too many hours as a house parent in an orphanage, teaching Sunday school, reading my Bible and praying, and attending church. I was exhausted physically, emotionally, and spiritually.

In late January of 1973, I received a copy of the newly published New English Bible in the mail. I started reading in Romans and was stunned when I arrived at 3:28: "For we consider that a person is declared righteous by faith apart from the works of the law." In that gracious moment, I felt a load roll off my shoulders. I realized that not only had I been originally saved by grace and called to vocational ministry by grace, but I was also to live by grace and minister by grace. I didn't have to go to church, read my Bible, pray, and tithe in order to impress God or even please God. Rather, I was invited to trust him on every level and do all those good things not to earn his favor but because I already *had* his favor.

If I had not experienced the rebirth of grace in my life, I would never have survived as a pastor. I would have operated as though my success as a pastor—measured numerically, of course—was essential to right standing with the Lord. There would be many other times during my four decades of ministry when I would have to relearn this lesson of grace on an even deeper level. I seemed to have a propensity to turn the gracious call of God to full-time vocational ministry into a path whereby I could earn favor.

The majority of my ministry has been carried out in fairly isolated places, such as Yankton, South Dakota, and Othello, Washington. I have often lacked close mentors who could nurture my call or help me grow as a human being, as a Christ follower, and as a pastor. I have come to believe that one of the greatest needs of pastors and those who are studying for the ministry is a healthy relationship with their peers. Too many good men and women who are called and gifted by God are falling by the wayside because they don't have supportive, nurturing friendships with fellow pastors. The call of God must include the fellowship of God's people.

I feel like my conversion, my Spirit-filling, and my call to ministry were all dramatic, life-changing, Damascus-road-type events in my life. Perhaps because of my own introversion and insecurities, the Lord needed to make my call clear and dramatic. That has tended to be the pattern in my life—to receive clear-cut guidance that calls me to follow or not and a clear-cut call to align my will with the will of God. It has been a grand adventure over these four decades. Not always easy or smooth sailing, but I wouldn't trade my life for anyone's life. Lou Gehrig isn't the only one who can say, "I consider myself the luckiest man on the face of the earth."

Rev. Dr. Jesse Middendorf
General Superintendent Emeritus
Church of the Nazarene
Overland Park, Kansas

My options were wide open. When I was a young boy, we often talked around the supper table about the expectation that an education was essential. But the future was not constrained or limited. My father, a pastor, was from a family of craftsmen, miners, carpenters, soldiers, engineers, and chemical workers. My mother, a schoolteacher, was from a family of attorneys, physicians, ministers, and military officers. The family relationships were warm, the exposure to the variety of careers and pursuits frequent, and the conversations in our home stoked our curiosity.

Dad's work as a pastor was his passion. His call was a subject of testimony and sermon and was frequently a topic of conversation in the home. Following God's will was the primary motive for life in our home, but knowing what that might mean was an open topic. I was challenged to study well and explore many life options but also to seek to know God's will, wherever that might lead.

My earliest interests were in aviation, and I found myself dreaming about becoming a pilot. The most intriguing option seemed to be naval aviation, and my imagination of flying from the deck of an aircraft carrier captivated my mind for several years. As I grew into adolescence, however, my interests shifted toward medicine—not without some sense that perhaps that might become a means of fulfilling a call to missions. That was an option that presented itself to me on several occasions when missionary doctors were guests in both our church and home. An uncle who had served as a missionary doctor added to the interest, and I was intrigued by the possibility of visiting other cultures.

My father served his entire ministry as a pastor in the Deep South—in Tennessee, Georgia, North Carolina, Mississippi, and Alabama. As I grew into adolescence, attending school in three of those states, I was often aware of the social fomentation beginning to occur. My father, a native of Missouri, was passionate about racial equality and fairness. I watched as, without fanfare, he took strong stands for racial equality in the church and the community. He was not a crusader, marching in the streets or engaging in protests, which were beginning to take root in the South. But he was unyielding in his insistence that no one was barred from attending church, whatever their race. He occasionally faced fierce resistance in the churches where he pastored, but he persisted with kindness and always with a strong insistence that the clear teaching of Scripture and the message of holiness of heart and life demanded that the church welcome *everyone*.

On one occasion I witnessed him being physically attacked for his stance. With a firm but kind insistence, he refused to give in or cower in the face of opposition. My values were deeply impacted by his quiet, nonjudgmental approach and his unwavering insistence that the church should lead the way in addressing social evil for the sake of the mission of God. For my dad, it was less about social change and more about evangelism and life transformation. He insisted this was the work of the church.

By the time I graduated from high school, a sense of call toward ministry in some form seemed to be a growing awareness. It was not so much a sudden knowing as much as a developing idea. My hunger to know God and to follow God's will in my life was constant and fed by godly parents and a succession of effective Sunday school teachers who formed in me a fascination for the Scriptures. I was a typical adolescent, however, and found myself often wrestling with my own stubborn will, my determination to make things conform to my expectations, and my desire to be accepted by my friends and classmates.

Having good friends who wanted to follow God's will was a gift I did not fully appreciate until looking back in later years. Those formative friendships helped build some protective hedges around me. Our pursuits as developing adolescents were not built around the destructive habits that consumed some of our peers. Rather, our lives were formed around involvement in high school musical organizations and sports activities and the constant involvement in local church and district activities that were high energy and engaging.

College opened new doors of opportunity to explore the options for where life might lead. I wrestled for some time over whether ministry, medicine, or aviation would be my life choice. During my time as a student at Trevecca Nazarene College (now University), there was a developing hunger to know God better and to know for certain where I should focus my attention.

During my college years, we as a nation endured the tragedy of the assassination of President John F. Kennedy. I was dating the lady who was later to become my wife. One day, as we ate lunch at a café near the campus, the owner suddenly brought out a small television set, putting it up on the counter so everyone could see and hear. To our utter shock and dismay, we heard the announcement that the president had been shot and declared dead. Our world was shaken. We had already been impacted by the Cuban Missile Crisis. A growing engagement of our military in a small country in southeastern Asia called Vietnam had created another reason for uneasiness. Friends from both high school and college had been drafted into the military, and I had been notified that my draft status had been changed. I began to wonder whether I would be able to complete my college education before the military called my number. In that milieu that I became aware of the extent to which we lived in a broken world.

Only months removed from that moment, we were traveling with the college choir, on the annual spring tour to visit local churches across the educational region. On that trip we visited Selma, Alabama. As we drove into town, the bus we were on was stopped at a roadblock by police and highway patrolmen. They demanded to know why our bus was headed into Selma. We finally were able to convince them that we really were a college choir from a Christian college, visiting a local church for a concert. Begrudgingly, they allowed us to drive in, but they insisted that the bus could not be parked in town overnight. As we drove into town, we drove past the burned-out hulk of another bus. The tension in the town was tangible. Worried faces everywhere stared at our bus, some with unmistakable anger. But we went ahead with the concert and sang to a full house. The church seemed genuinely relieved to be able to have a normal Sunday morning service.

My life began to take a new turn. I became convinced that the message of Jesus Christ was the only adequate resource for a nation seemingly at war with itself. While I was deeply convinced that the world at large was in desperate need of the gospel, I grew in the conviction that the nation of my birth was going through deep social upheaval. I did not know how to articulate what I sensed, but I became convicted that my role was to be a pastor, serving not only a congregation but making a difference in a community, a city, and—as far as possible—the nation.

Many of us wrestled with what we were seeing, hearing, and experiencing in the dormitory rooms. Some were staunchly against the "rabble" who were creating unrest in the nation. Their interpretation of a solution was that we needed strong police forces who would deal forcefully with dissenters and bring about the social stability that would maintain the status quo. Others were convinced that social change was not only desirable but absolutely necessary to the survival of the nation. The tension in our dorm rooms was sometimes high, and the debates in many of our classes were intense, loud, and occasionally somewhat disruptive. But the sense that increasingly grew in my heart was that my life's work was clear. Ministry as a pastor was the call of God.

The years of college and seminary education were formative at deep and profound levels for me. I studied for ministry in the midst of the social upheaval that characterized the 1960s. Godly professors, pastors, and mentors shaped my understanding of the call to ministry. My father, whose pastoral service began at the dawn of World War II, encouraged my pursuit of the call but expressed his concern that my call be clear and that I not merely pattern my life after his. He wanted me to know that the load would be heavy, the cost could be high, and that there were many obstacles to overcome. But he also assured me that if this was God's will, it would be the most fulfilling life I could ever imagine.

I married the daughter of a godly layman. Life-deep in a local church and heavily involved in the district and general church, he became a fervent encourager, friend, and supporter. Marrying Susan Marlowe provided me with a support system that fully complemented the family system in which I grew up. It was a divine guidance for which I have been eternally grateful.

I could never have imagined where the journey of ministry would take us. Serving as a pastor was most fulfilling. God led us into relationships with people, churches, and communities that shaped us. My service as an administrator offered challenges and opportunities that were beyond my abilities and far beyond my expectation. But godly men and women surrounded my life in many ways.

In my service as a general superintendent, I came into an even deeper appreciation for the call of God into Christian ministry. As I ordained women and men around the globe, often asking to hear their story of the call of God, I was often deeply moved by the conviction that God still calls women and men into ministry. No two stories are alike. No two journeys are the same. God does not make carbon copies. Every minister and every minister's story is an original. God's plan, from the beginning, was that God would utilize the gifts and abilities of people as the means of fulfilling God's purposes in the world.

Some things, once you know them, change everything. Once you know that God has called, nothing will ever be the same again. And nothing could be better than saying yes!

LAYING THE FOUNDATION

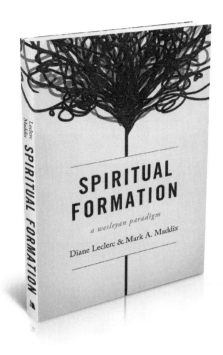

There is an increased interest in spirituality in our world lately. People have a deep hunger and thirst for the transcendent.

In *Spiritual Formation,* Maddix and Leclerc provide a definition of Christian spiritual formation within the Wesleyan paradigm and assist faithful disciples in deepening their relationships with Jesus Christ. The book focuses on how people can grow in Christlikeness by participating in Scripture reading, the sacraments, and other spiritual disciplines.

Spiritual Formation
Diane Leclerc & Mark A. Maddix, Editors
ISBN: 978-0-8341-2613-8

BEACON HILL PRESS
OF KANSAS CITY
Available online at BeaconHillBooks.com

"Brilliantly conceived, thoroughly engrossing, and thought-provoking from first to last."

— Dr. Leonard Sweet

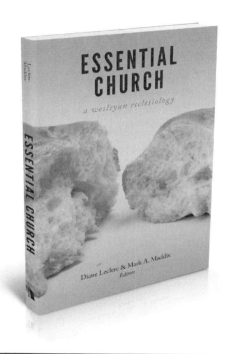

With so many denominations and differing ideas about what the church is and does, arriving at a clear understanding of the church is a formidable challenge.

The pastors and educators who have contributed to this book explore the meaning, purpose, and function of the church, as well as its structure. They address topics such as the kingdom of God, worship, and mission in relation to the body of Christ, and give special attention to Wesleyan theological concerns.

ssential Church
iane Leclerc & Mark A. Maddix, Editors
BN: 978-0-8341-3242-9

BEACON HILL PRESS
OF KANSAS CITY

Available online at BeaconHillBooks.com